LITTLE BOOK OF THE
ORIENT EXPRESS

LITTLE BOOK OF THE
ORIENT
EXPRESS

First published in the UK in 2012

© Demand Media Limited 2012

www.demand-media.co.uk

Printed and bound in China

ISBN 978-1-909217-23-2

Contents

The Birth of the World's Most Famous Train

In the eighteenth century, the roads, as well as the breed of horses, had progressed to the extent that heavy carriages could be dragged over long distances. However, it still remained impossible to take heavy goods along the roads except in perfect weather – and even then the carriage speed was rarely more than three miles an hour.

River and canal traffic was as important a means of transportation as roads but was unable to satisfy the ever-growing needs of industry and commerce. Mail coaches carried travellers but even the shortest of journeys was uncomfortable and sometimes a precarious journey.

On 27 September 1825, the world's first railroad worked by a steam locomotive was opened between the towns of Stockton and Darlington in the north east of England, covering a distance of 11 miles. This development heralded the beginning of an era of massive social and technological progress. In a period of just over 25 years the communication system of the entire civilised world was revolutionised.

In that time, the 11 miles of track progressed to six thousand in Britain, while in Europe, France opened its first railroad in 1832, Belgium in 1835, Austria and Prussia in 1838 and Spain in 1848. By 1840, trains were running on nearly 3,000 miles of American

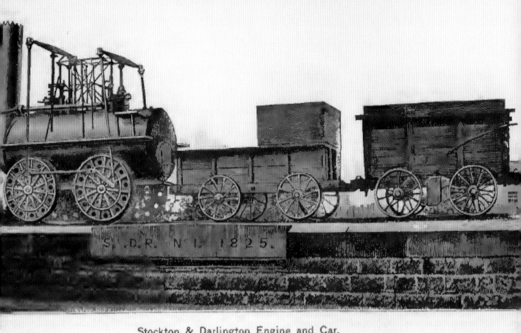

Stockton & Darlington Engine and Car.

track, where the general aim was to get a railroad running at the maximum rate of progress and at the minimum cost.

Passenger cars were primarily not much more than stagecoaches chained together behind a locomotive, but as the railroads were extended and linked together; journeys of several hundred miles became a regular occurrence. It was now essential to provide some form of comfort, plus protection from the weather.

The open passenger car on US railroads was characteristic of a country devoted to a democratic way of life, as opposed to the British carriages not to mention the ones on continental Europe, both of which featured small compartments to separate the social classes.

Georges Nagelmackers

The railroads had come of age. Those European railroad managers and engineers who were not prejudiced about the New World opportunism began to study the innovations developed in America. And one man, a young Belgian called Georges Nagelmackers, was one of the few who admired the dynamic enterprise in America. Born in 1845 in Liege, Nagelmackers was passionate about railroads and he decided not to match the Americans but to score off them.

With the exception of Britain, Belgium had the best designed and most efficiently managed network of railroads in Europe. It was this superb and innovative system that struck a chord with the young Belgian and set him on a course that would change the way the world viewed luxury train travel and one train in particular.

Nagelmackers' father was heavily involved in railroad finance and the family's social prestige and wealth ensured personal friendship with the King, and subsequently with the King's relatives in virtually every ruling dynasty in Europe. Nagelmackers' character was that of an entrepreneur and as an almost inevitable result of his childhood spent watching primitive trains steaming off to distant places, his thoughts turned to visions of the fortunes being made during that era of railroad mania.

His main thought couldn't have been bigger: a train that would span a continent and for more than 1,500 miles. What was truly incredible about this ambition was that he was 20 years old when he had it.

To cross Europe from west to east in the mid-1800s was an odyssey only contemplated by gypsies and military leaders. Those who had to travel from one end of the continent to the other undertook most of the journey by sea. But as this resourceful young man was quick to highlight to his father when the idea was discussed, every European country, big or small, had been constructing railroads for prestige, industrial expansion, profit and future military use. As such, he could sense a realistic opportunity.

Cautiously, Georges' father told him that international cooperation between the many European railroad companies

would be improbable and that financial investment would be risky. But his father also knew that his son had an ace up his sleeve: their principal client, debtor and fellow railroad buff, was none other than Leopold II, who had just succeeded his father as the king of Belgium.

Georges said to his father: 'With the King's name formally linked with the business, not only will we get the required finance but the necessary engineering work and running facilities will be approved by the stockholders anxious to see the enterprise succeed.'

Unforeseen obstacles and opportunities

Unfortunately, Nagelmackers' grand plan took an unexpected turn at this point, one which would – ironically – derail the *Orient Express* birth for some time: he fell in love. His object of desire was 10 years his senior, but sadly for Georges his love was not returned and he took this rejection extremely hard.

He abandoned all interest in his railroad project and on the suggestion of his father, took a vacation in a destination as far away as he could conveniently go – America.

His trip to New York was a revelation to him. He saw the country as a land of opportunity and nothing impressed him more than the nation's railroads; long journeys, which involved days of travel, were now commonplace.

Fascinated by schedules that listed a myriad of towns, Georges travelled all over the country, enjoying the new experience of big passenger cars built as saloons, without compartments

and decked out with mirrors, carved woodwork and ingenious methods of turning the upholstered seats into sleeping bunks for travel at night-time.

A long, heavy car was essential for the luxury, transcontinental train he had dreamed of. And it was here in America that he saw the proof of how viable such a train could be.

The stimulus to forget his emotional troubles and to transform his dreams into reality came on a daily basis. He read in the newspapers of the fantastic scheme to bind the young nation together with a band of steel from coast to coast. Lincoln's vision of a Pacific Railroad began in July 1865, a link between the Union and the Central Pacific in the desolate terrain north of the Great Salt Lake.

But the historic completion of this was still four years away but the confident notion that it would be completed was manna from heaven to Nagelmackers.

George Mortimer Pullman

He was no engineer, but Nagelmackers was fascinated by the mechanical ingenuity of experts. But what interested him even more were the stories about the man who was regarded as the sleeping-car king of America – George Mortimer Pullman.

Born in New York, one of a family of 10 children, Pullman was selling farm implements by the age of 14. However, eight years later, while travelling the four-hour, 58-mile journey to Buffalo, the idea of building luxury saloon cars for railroad travel came to him. However, after the death of his father, he took over the family business and all dreams were placed firmly on hold.

His luck was to change when the general store he ran in Gregory Gulch during the Civil War began to turn a more than tidy profit, so much so that he had enough capital to move to Chicago with approximately $20,000 and the chance to gamble the entire sum on building the first Pullman car.

By the time the work was finished he was nearly down to his last dollar. The car was named *Pioneer*. Its décor became the theme that prevailed in every luxury train coach for nearly a century.

After a sales pitch of quite brazen yet impressive levels, Pullman saw *Pioneer* given the privileged honour of being the funeral train for the recently assassinated US President, Abraham Lincoln. This was far from the end of Pullman's moment in the public eye, as General Ulysees S. Grant was the recipient of another Pullman offer, this time to travel in his luxurious car for a hero's journey back to his hometown in Illinois after engineering victory in the Civil War.

Georges Nagelmackers was among the thousands who inspected *Pioneer* and as a distinguished foreign visitor was invited to enjoy a free trip. Accustomed to the heavy décor and lavish use of high quality woods, brass and gold leaf in European chateaux and stately homes, he was not overly impressed with the interior. What impressed him was that such a weight was possible for a train of several cars. The same amount of cars he had envisaged for the *Orient Express*. He was even more interested in the structural side.

Pullman gave Nagelmackers the run of his workshops and proudly displayed

Left: George Pullman.

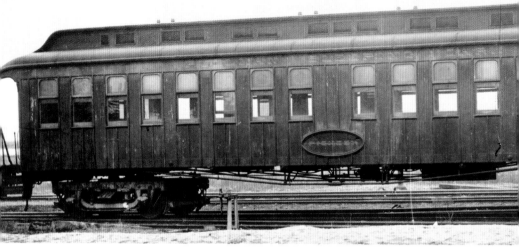

Above: *Pioneer.*

contracts that gave him a monopoly of running his cars over thousands of miles of railroads, passing from one company's tracks to another without hindrance. This through-running facility was the feature of the Pullman enterprise that impressed Nagelmackers the most.

He memorised the legal jargon of all of the contracts, knowing the knowledge would be invaluable once he tackled the main problem of persuading the independent and cautious European railroad enterprises to give him overriding control of a special train, including when and where it ran, at what speed and what fare could be charged.

The bait he decided to use was that

he would supply the cars at no cost to the railroads. They would not only enjoy the prestige of the finest train in Europe servicing their routes but they would take all of the basic passenger fares as well. Nagelmackers on the other hand, would bank the supplementary charge for each passenger and whatever could be gained by providing meals, drinks and extra luxuries.

Georges spent just over a year in America and once home he recounted everything he had learned to his impressed father. They reminded each other of the intention to get King Leopold involved and went off to meet him.

Finance aside, the king was genuinely interested in Georges' description of

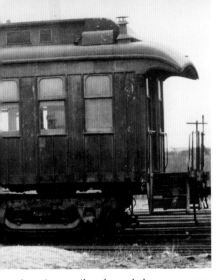

American railroads and he was eager to further the status of Belgium as a leading railroad country in Europe. He agreed that his name could head a list of subscribers, plus he signed a letter of recommendation for Georges. The new company of Nagelmackers et Cie was born, and the company proposed as its initial venture, to organise a luxury train to run from Paris to Berlin.

There was just one problem. Neither Georges nor the king realised that war between France and Germany was imminent. By the start of 1870, the cars were ready and hauled to Liege, where King Leopold inspected them. However, on 19 July, France declared war on Prussia.

For a man less determined than Georges Nagelmackers this would have been the end of the enterprise, but he refused to abandon his idea. He acquired an unrivalled knowledge of the network of European railroads and he designed a route from Ostend in neutral Belgium to Brindisi on the heel of Italy.

Plus, both conflicting nations were anxious not to arouse the anger of the British by attacking a small nation ruled by a close relative of Queen Victoria. And Britain was soon to prove the best customer for the new train. The success of this new route was short lived due to the obstacle created by the French who rejected Nagelmackers' application to travel through the Mont Cenis tunnel through the Alps.

But he remained as determined as ever. He made a new start, re-registering his enterprise under the name to become world-famous: La Compagnie Internationale des Wagon-Lits. His fortunes didn't exactly change for the better, though. In fact this depressing stage in his career saw him almost cut his losses and he settled into a safe but mundane banking career. But the brink of success was just round the corner.

THE BIRTH OF THE WORLD'S MOST FAMOUS TRAIN

Colonel William d'Alton Mann

The first hint of Nagelmackers' future prosperity came in a cordial letter inviting him to travel to London to discuss matters of "mutual commercial interest". The invitation was signed by Colonel William d'Alton Mann, an American with a reputation for unconventional business methods sufficient to make any banker shudder. However, he also boasted an infectious charisma and considerable self-confidence.

Mann had decided that Europe's train services were due for his attention and he had heard of a young Belgian banker with an enthusiasm for railroads and more importantly, with all the right contacts with Europe's most influential families. In short, Mann thought Nagelmackers the appropriate partner to help him eclipse Pullman as the overlord of the railroads.

The American was staying at a luxury suite in London's Langham Hotel. At the time he set up his business in London he was in his mid-thirties, but had a dubious business career behind him. However,

Mann's military legacy was one of incredible achievement. The youngest colonel in the Union army, he was placed under the command of General George A. Custer.

But after his unit endured a heavy mauling he left the command of his regiment and resigned. However, his military experience had not been unprofitable. He had taken the clever idea to patent various ideas of his own to improve horse trappings and cavalrymen's equipment, selling the design to the War Department as a patriotic if financially appealing enterprise. With this newly achieved capital he went into oil exploration.

Unfortunately, success in this area eluded him, to the extent that he was arrested for fraud. He managed to evade punishment on technicalities and declared himself bankrupt. This led to his next venture as, of all things, a tax collector, in Mobile, Alabama, where he ended up a massively popular figure but one investigated for even greater financial improprieties.

He turned his attention to railroads. He moved to New York where he boasted about the impressive engineering feat and prosperous new railroad he had launched that ran between New Orleans, Mobile and Chattanooga. It was in New York where he officially joined the exclusive echelon of the railroad tycoon. It was then that he decided to go into direct competition with none other than George Pullman.

He failed to beat Pullman in direct competition but he did manage to make a good profit by building private railroad cars for the business magnates. His greatest coup was in fact building a special car for Lillie Langtry, the English vaudeville star. When she arrived in America she had a rapturous reception and rode in state down Fifth Avenue. It was Colonel Mann who got the contract to provide a railroad coach for her tour through the country and the money rolled in.

This meant Mann had sufficient money to go to the expense of shipping two of his boudoir cars to England, where they could be inspected by prospective customers. He invited journalists and British railways directors to lavish receptions at the Langham Hotel and scores of society's most prominent people came to his parties. However, the European railroad experts were unenthusiastic about what he could offer, except one: Georges Nagelmackers.

Georges fell for Mann's patter completely and accepted every proposal Mann threw at him. Nagelmackers' Compagnie International became a subsidiary of the Mann Company and Georges was persuaded to step down from the position of senior manager.

At first things went well. A masterstroke from Mann saw him offer the use of one of his boudoir cars to the Prince of Wales, who was to represent Britain at the wedding of his brother Alfred to Marie Alexandrovna, the only daughter of Czar Alexander II in St Petersburg. The car would take the Prince from the English Channel port through France and Germany to Russia. This scoop paid off so satisfactorily that Pullman quickly launched a separate company to build and run Pullman cars in Europe.

Unfortunately, as a result of Pullman's resources and available cars, Mann and Georges were faced with severe obstacles to get any of their cars into operation. As Mann's methods descended from underhand to the morally reprehensible, Nagelmackers couldn't stomach his business partner any longer and offered to buy him out. Mann agreed and sold out his interests for $5 million to his partner and a cartel of financiers and returned to New York.

The rebirth of Compagnie Internationale des Wagon-Lits

The original company was reinstituted under its old name and Leopold II once more allowed his name to head the list of chief subscribers. In the inaugural year of the company, 1876, Nagelmackers would travel extensively to negotiate and secure new contracts.

He inspected the royal train of Ludwig II of Bavaria on his travels and was impressed with the degree of luxury money could buy. However, all of the railroad directors were of the opinion that such opulence was not for anyone of non-regal blood, even if they were wealthy, so all Georges could secure were short-term contracts.

Nagelmackers' expresses ran between Paris and Vienna, Paris and Cologne, Paris and Menton, Vienna and Munich and Ostend and Berlin. His new standard and bigger cars (plus his restaurant car) were well patronised,

which amazed the railroad companies. But Nagelmackers was still far from achieving his vision of running a complete luxury train across Europe.

The route from the English Channel ports to the borders of the Black Sea was now technically feasible; it was commercially where he met with a wall of resistance. Railroad companies were adamant that an independent company without a mile of track to its name would not run an international express on the established tracks.

However, persistence plus Leopold II's encouragement to his royal relatives to exert pressure where a company was privately owned, not to mention the suggestion that they calculate their own profits where they could benefit from state railroads, slowly broke down the objections of the companies.

By May 1883, Nagelmackers had conducted agreements that included the Wagon-Lits Compagnie and the Imperial Railways of Alsace-Lorraine, the Royal Romanian Railways and the Grand Duchy of Baden State Railways.

The route he selected ran from Paris through Munich, Salzburg, Vienna, Budapest, and Bucharest to Giurgiu, which formed the border between

Romania and Bulgaria. Ships would ferry passengers across the river to Ruschuk and a special Bulgarian train would take the rest of the passengers booked for Istanbul as far as Varna on the Black Sea coast.

Eastbound, the scheduled time from Paris to Istanbul was 81 hours, 40 minutes; westbound it was 77 hours and 49 minutes. The sheer exactness of Nagelmackers' projections a sublime example of the lengths to which he would go to ensure that his train would be seen a paragon of efficiency.

Interestingly, despite all of his impressive organisational skills and forethought, one particular issue had not been addressed by Nagelmackers, the name of the train itself. However, it was being dubbed the *Orient Express* in the newspapers and so Nagelmackers decided to use this exciting moniker as the train's title when it made its first ever run in October 1883.

Centre: Sirkeci station in Istanbul - inaugurated as the terminus of the *Orient Express*.

The Maiden Journey

Far Right:
Georges
Nagelmackers,
The *Orient Express*
founder.

The official inaugural journey of the *Orient Express*, scheduled for 4 October 1883, had caught the public's imagination. Parisians had become incredibly excited by the press stories describing the train's luxurious nature, the exotic foods and the list of distinguished people who would be travelling on the train. The most colourful headline exclaimed that the train was: 'The Magic Carpet to the Orient.'

However, the stories proclaiming this the train's first run were not entirely truthful as there had been several trial runs of the Wagon-Lits cars, the first a year earlier. The reason for the delay was that Nagelmackers had to engage in months of negotiations with several governments (and in some cases authorise pay-offs to senior officials) to ensure that the route to Bulgaria was secured.

In fact for six years after the first journey, passengers had to disembark in Serbia and cross the mountain in bone-shaking transport to the Turkish railhead at Tatar Paazardzhik.

But for the inaugural journey, Nagelmackers did not dare to inflict such an exasperating route on his guests. The train would travel as far as Giurgiu in Romania, before passengers would have to cross the Danube by ferry to Ruschuk. From here, passengers would travel by a special train Nagelmackers had borrowed from the Austrian State Railways to the Bulgarian port of Vanna.

The trip would continue aboard an Austrian packed boat across the Black Sea to the Turkish capital.

However, Nagelmackers had decided to keep this improvised route completely secret. Each and every passenger believed that they would be taking the new luxury train all the way to Istanbul. In short, he was taking a massive risk.

When the evening arrived the ever-shrewd Nagelmackers had even arranged for several of the aging Mann boudoir cars, unwashed and with peeling pain, to be lined up on the adjacent track. The contrast with the sparking exterior of the *Orient Express* would be dramatic.

First to arrive was Nagelmackers himself, alongside Napoleon Schroeder,

his French representative, Delloye-Matthieu, the president of the Compagnie des Wagon-Lits, Etienne Lechat, one of the train's financial backers and several of the company's directors. The Belgians, invited to stress that this was a Belgian enterprise as well as an international occasion, included the Minister of Public Works, the manager of the Belgian State Railways, and several members of the Wagon-Lits board.

The French party boasted 19 guests, including the son of the Minister of Posts and Communications, while the Ottoman Empire was represented by its Paris *charge d'affaires*, Mishal Effendi. The many journalists invited to report on the journey included two of the best-known writers of the time: Edmond About (regarded as one of the earliest science-fiction writers) and Henri Opper de Blowitz, *The Times*' Paris correspondent.

The book About subsequently produced, *De Pontoise a Stamboul*, remains the most vivid and reasonably accurate account of the first official *Orient Express* journey.

A modernised version of the original Buddicom engine and built in 1878 was selected by Nagelmackers as his locomotive for the maiden journey. It was in the class known as 500 and was equipped with the pumping apparatus for the Westinghouse compressed air braking system. Immediately behind the locomotive tender was a six-wheel covered truck which carried mail, the only source of revenue on the inaugural run.

There followed two sleeping cars, each with accommodation for 20 passengers, and a restaurant car, with it gleaming glassware and silver cutlery. At the rear was a four-wheel fourgon loaded with the passengers' baggage, containers of food and crates of wine, champagne, port, brandy and liqueurs. Nagelmackers had insisted on being ready for the gastronomic delights with which his guests were to be spoilt.

Nagelmackers had also ensured that first-class service would be something that his train would be renowned for, not just on the first journey but on what he hoped would be the many to come. A special school was established and the first instructors were *maitre d'hôtel* and banqueting managers recruited from luxury hotels. Over the years the corps of the Compagnie employees grew into a hierarchy, within which promotion was as strictly regulated as in a government service.

The *chef de train* was the commander in chief, the *contrôleur* was his deputy. Then came *the chefs de brigades*, the *conducteurs*, the *brigadier-postiers* and *bagagistes* and finally the *bagagistes-nettoyeurs* (the porters and the cleaners). The manager of the restaurant was titled the *maitre d'hôtel* and under him were the *serveurs-receveurs* (headwaiters who supervised the service and presented the bills), followed by various grades of waiters. Likewise, there was a kitchen hierarchy from the chef de cuisine to humble kitchen help, such as

plongeurs (dishwashers) and cleaners.

To the annoyance of the engineers damping down the locomotive's fire and to the *chef de train*, the guests continued to chat and procrastinate despite the pleas of the stationmaster, and their departure time of 6pm came and went. When everyone had finally been escorted on board, the train rather jerkily steamed off to cheers from the crowd of spectators.

Local trains had been held on branch lines to give the train a clear run and it made up for the lost 20 minutes long before it reached Strasbourg. The train was exceeding 55mph on the straight sections.

Meantime, About, a man with a reputation as an arbiter of taste, was making copious notes in compartment seven (soon to become famous as the permanently arranged accommodation for the train's most regular VIP, the arms king, Basil Zaharoff, more of whom in chapter six), and his companion was Turkish diplomat Mishak Effendi. He eulogised about the train's interior, which was, in truth, the reaction of all of the passengers on board.

From the teak and mahogany panelling of the compartment walls and car doors to the deep armchairs covered in Spanish leather, About was enthralled.

Left: Edmond About.

Right: The wealthy US railroad enthusiast who inspired Nagelmacker.

In fact, despite the cold temperature of the train's first ever autumn evening, he was even impressed with the heating system on board. That said, both About and his fellow passengers' state of warmth and tranquillity was no doubt helped by the copious amounts of fine wine and alcohol on board.

The self-appointed publicist of the train was also greatly impressed by the train's dining rooms, insisting that they 'took his breath away', with a décor that definitely bore witness to the grandiose taste of the Victorian age. Lit by huge gas chandeliers, the dining rooms were breathtaking in their finery and became symbolic of the *Orient Express*: think of the train and no doubt the indelible image of these rooms is potentially the first thing that you think about.

At precisely 8pm, the *conducteurs* knocked at the compartment doors and announced that dinner would be served 15 minutes later. Snow-white damask cloths adorned the tables and at each place sat four glasses of the finest Baccarat crystal from Louis XVI's famous Luneville factory. The cutlery was solid silver, the plates of finest porcelain.

The sumptuous feasts lasted nearly three hours. From time to time, Nagelmackers and his directors got up and stopped at some of the tables to exchange pleasantries with guests.

The train pulled into Strasbourg station, 300 miles from Paris, shortly before dawn, in perfect time for the official reception. The European president of the American Edison Company, Mr Porges, was waiting with his engineers to show the train's guests around the plant. Only four people emerged, the rest (including About and Opper de Blowitz) remained in their sleeping compartments unaware even of the change of locomotives.

In fact, such was their enjoyment and their state of utter relaxation that they stayed in their compartments for the rest of the run, via Karlsruhe, Ulm and Munich to Vienna.

One such incident perfectly summarises just how organised Nagelmackers was, and in turn how prepared the train was for every eventuality. Just before the train reached Munich, black smoke began to penetrate the crevices in the floor of the kitchen and corridor of the restaurant car.

The train was stopped while Nagelmackers himself led the locomotive engineers, the fireman, and three of the train's guards to inspect the damage. He persuaded the engineer to take the train slowly as far as Munich, 30 miles away, where the resourceful Nagelmackers had arranged to have another restaurant car standing in reserve. The entire time, the passengers were unaware of the danger that a fire could have broken out.

And so the train crossed the Austro-Bavarian border and its capital Vienna, 270 miles from Munich. The reception there was akin to a state occasion and included Emperor Franz Josef. The passengers were escorted to the station restaurant where a champagne supper was served. A tour had also been organised to visit the International Exhibition of Electric Lighting, held to display the latest developments in illumination by the American Edison Company and the German firm Siemens.

Unfortunately, the majority of the passengers it had been intended to impress were fast asleep in their compartments, including both Opper de Blowitz, who again missed this arranged event.

After breakfast, Nagelmackers toured the train to announce that in a few minutes they would be drawing into Budapest station. 'The *Orient Express*

has now travelled 1,500 kilometres since we left Paris,' he proudly informed his passengers. He was in fact understating the distance; it was in fact 1,048 miles, equivalent to 1,671 kilometres.

For many, arriving in Budapest was the first glimpse of a place tinged with the atmosphere of the East. The train eased gently over the bridge, and once it had crossed from Buda into Pest, the train's leisurely pace ensured that it had arrived in time for the formal reception to be held mid-morning, where a lavish buffet had been prepared for all of the guests.

The banquet positively teamed with delicious, rich food and whether, after the train resumed its journey, the passengers sat down and were able to take lunch, is not a matter of record.

The empire's final gesture to the *Orient Express* had been secretly arranged in cooperation with Nagelmackers during the Vienna stop. When the train came to a halt at the station in Szegedin, an ancient city standing at the confluence of the Tisza and Maros rivers, a band of Hungarian gypsies came dancing along the street toward the station. They were playing flutes, fiddles, tambourines and drums. The leader, explaining to

THE MAIDEN JOURNEY

Nagelmackers that he was the king of the gypsies, was invited along with his troupe onto the train.

The lively music burst out as the train set off once more. For the next 70 miles, the music played on, until the train reached Temesvar (now Timisoara in Romania). Some of the diplomats and journalists danced around the confined space. When the musicians launched into their version of *La Marseillaise*, the *chef de cuisine* began to sing. Finally, with enthusiasm for the country he regarded as his adopted motherland along with England, de Blowitz, joined in the singing, waving his hat in the air.

After a brief stop at the border, the train was in Romania and the Balkans, the fifth country of the itinerary, and for many this was now an expedition into the unknown. And as the train entered the Transylvanian Alps, de Blowitz was coming into his own.

Using his own ancestry as a descendent of a legendary Bohemian count as a way of introducing himself, he began interviewing many of the European statesmen on board. The fact they he had never previously travelled in Romania did not prevent him from implying that the remote

country passing before the windows revived memories of his youth. As the *Orient Express* entered the Balkan countries, de Blowitz was convinced every mile took him nearer to yet more journalistic scoops, which would include interviews with King Charles and Sultan Abdul Hamid.

Before nightfall, the passengers were

Romanian king was arranged. This trip lasted several hours and by the time the passengers had rejoined the *Orient Express* many were exhausted.

When the passengers woke up the train was slowly travelling on towards Bulgaria and leaving the Transylvanian Alps behind. Seven hours after leaving Bucharest, the train stopped at Giurgiu, a truly miserable place. Here, the passengers had to leave the comfort of the train for a small steamship which would ferry them across the wide river to the Bulgarian border post of Ruschuk.

Once on board the train again, the *Orient Express* steamed on to the Black Sea port of Varna, through a barren and unwelcoming countryside. Before the train reached Sheytandijk, the passengers were told by the car attendants that they were passing through bandit country. Lunch was served on arrival at the station, and to combat the cold temperatures and rising impatience of the guests, due to a poor main course, Nagelmackers ensured there were many bottles of wine and brandy to assuage even the most vexed of passengers.

At long last the train pulled into Varna (the Odessus of ancient Greece) on the edge of the Black Sea. Apart

able to view the Iron Gates, between the southern end of the Carpathian Mountains and the Miroch range of the Balkan Mountains. Progress was slow and bumpy and the stretch from the Iron Gates to Bucharest took some seven hours.

When the train finally arrived a memorable excursion to meet the

Centre:
Timisoara.

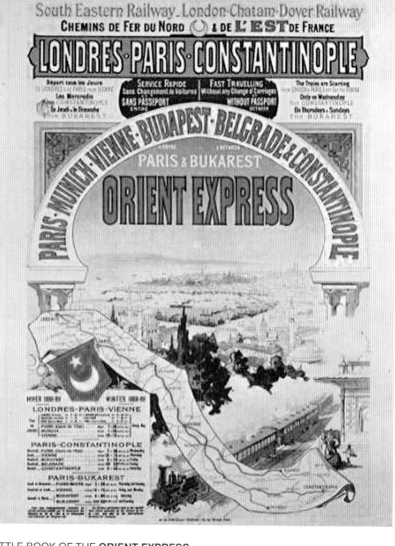

from beggars and officials no one seemed to take much notice of this historic occasion as the passengers from Paris were marshalled by Nagelmackers and his staff to the jetty, where a steamboat, the *Espero*, was in readiness to take the party to Istanbul.

The boat had left Trieste three weeks earlier and showed signs of the battering it had endured in stormy conditions. About was relieved that ropes and a timber barrier isolated the refugees on the deck. 'We kept mostly to our cabins,' he reported. The ship left Varna as dusk was falling and the passage to the Golden Horn in the centre of Istanbul – a distance of 170 miles, took more than 14 hours.

The *Espero* entered the Bosporus Strait just as dawn broke. This was an experience none of the passengers had wanted to miss. Everyone left their cabins to watch the panorama on each side of the 19-mile strait separating Europe from Asia. While the boat was manoeuvred to the quayside, the passengers savoured the majestic scene before them. Ahead was the stunning Basilica of St Sophia, while the six graceful minarets and awe-inspiring dome of the Blue Mosque garnered

nothing but wonder and awe.

The *Orient Express* party was greeted by the Belgian ambassador and a crowd of Turkish officials. Horse-drawn carriages were waiting to take the visitors to the Grand Hotel of Pera, and as they journeyed all the sights of this incredible city, from the column of Istanbul to the Topkapi, were presented before them.

After a memorable stay at their hotel, Nagelmackers and his party again embarked on the *Espero* on the afternoon of 13 October. Arriving at Varna before dawn the next morning, they were back in the comfort of the *Orient Express* cars late that afternoon.

For the now seasoned travellers, the return journey was uneventful. Thanks to the efforts of the Austrian, German and French railroad managements, any lost time was made up and the train halted in the Gare de l'Est in Paris precisely on schedule, at 6pm.

The celebrations were not over, however. Nagelmackers wanted to express his gratitude to his guests for accepting his hospitality and wanted everyone to enjoy one last dinner together. And with that, About would write, 'Eleven wonderful days of a unique and historic journey were over.'

Centre: *Orient Express* historic routes.

London

Calais

Paris

Strasbou

Zürich

Lausanne
Simplon

Mila

Orient-Express (1883–1914, 1919–1939, 1945–19••
with connection over water in the Black Sea until

Simplon-Orient-Express (1919-1939, 1945-1962),
then Direct-Orient-Express (until 1977)

Arlberg-Orient-Express (1930-1939, 1945-1962)

Venice-Simplon-Orient-Express (1982-2005)

ÖBB EN 262/263 Orient-Express (Paris-Budapest 1
Paris-Vienna 2001-2007; Strasbourg-Vienna 2007

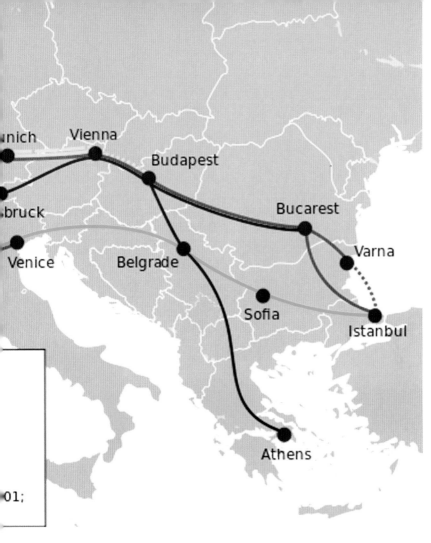

Munich

Vienna

Budapest

Innsbruck

Bucarest

Venice

Belgrade

Varna

Sofia

Istanbul

Athens

01;

From the Beginning to the Journey's End

From 1889, the *Orient Express* ran daily from the French capital to Budapest. It also had a timetable that mapped a route from Belgrade to Istanbul three times a week as well as travelling as far as the Black Sea once a week. While the name of the train remained constant, the route evolved over time.

In 1900, a new timetable was introduced which saw the *Orient Express* run daily from Paris to Budapest, three times a week to Istanbul via Belgrade and twice weekly via Constanta in Romania, and a special connection was opened via Salonika to Athens. Nagelmackers was also planning a Silver Jubilee celebration of his enterprise,

which was to take place in 1908.

Unfortunately, he did not live to see the event, as he died of a heart attack on 10 July 1905, two weeks after his sixtieth birthday. His death, undoubtedly caused by sheer overwork, was a sad blow not only to the Compagnie but to the world's railroad system, which he had revolutionised within two decades.

However, he left the Compagnie in the safe hands of Davison Dalziel, an English entrepreneur who was originally Nagelmackers' chief rival as managing director of the British Pullman Car Company. Eventually, the two companies combined and it was after Nagelmackers' death that he became the president of the Wagon-

Lits Compagnie while remaining the chairman of the Pullman Car Company.

In fact, the partnership between Nagelmackers and Dalziel was also cemented by a matrimonial linking of their families. Nagelmackers' only son Rene married Dalziel's only daughter Elizabeth in 1903.

Dalziel, until his death in 1928, greatly expanded the business of the two companies in many directions. In 1906, the Simplon tunnel under the Swiss Alps had been opened for traffic to Italy. Almost immediately thereafter the Compagnie organised a Wagon-Lits service between Paris and Venice via Lausanne and Milan. In 1912 it was extended to Trieste and provided an extremely fast service.

The Simplon *Orient Express* would signify an impressive shift in the Compagnie's strategy and its legacy would be forever secured when Agatha Christie set her masterpiece of mystery, *Murder on the Orient Express*, on the Simplon *Orient Express*.

The years before the First World War were the heyday for the original *Orient Express*, carrying VIPs and royalty through eighteenth century kingdoms on the finest carriages of the day. Unfortunately, when the Great War began in 1914, services were suspended, as it was widely recognised that steam locomotives were not particularly good for fighting

Above: Paris to Budapest route.

Centre: Avoiding Germany route.

the enemy in the same way that aircraft and vehicles that could travel anywhere were.

The train was operational again at the end of hostilities in 1918 (in fact the *Orient Express*' carriage 2419 was used

by the Allies as the venue for Germany to sign the Armistice to end the First World War) and was now routed via Milan when the opening of the Simplon Tunnel the following year allowed an alternative train ride. This service ran

in conjunction with the original routes and the Simplon *Orient Express* became the most important route between Paris and Istanbul.

Early in 1923, much of the panning and organisation to provide a regular service with the Simplon *Orient Express* crumbled when French and Belgian troops occupied the Ruhr as retaliation for Germany's failure to pay war reparations. Germany refused to handle the train on any part of her territory.

Far Right: The
Orient Express
heading towards
the coast.

Consequently a new route was devised through Basle and Zurich and using the Arlberg tunnel into Austria; thus was born the Arlberg *Orient Express*.

But it was the 1930s that were to prove the most important time for the steam locomotive and its services. By now there were many trains taking different routes and it became a haven for the rich and famous and renowned for its quality service, fine cuisine and the introduction of sleeping cars.

By 1932 the original *Orient Express* was restored with through cars from Paris to Istanbul (the new name for Constantinople since 1930); the Arlberg *Orient Express* maintained the service to Athens, the Simplon was routed to serve Belgrade, Sofia and Bucharest, while the Ostend-Vienna-*Orient Express* linked both the Belgian seaside resort with Vienna and connected the Austrian capital with the *Orient Express* for Bucharest and Istanbul.

During the winter of 1938, the Simplon *Orient Express* continued to run from Paris to Athens and Istanbul avoiding Germany. This lasted until the end of the "phony war" when Hitler attacked the Low Countries and brought France to its knees.

The onset of the Second World War once again saw services shut down and not resumed until the end of the conflict 1945.

It was during the Second World War that Germany, in the form of Hitler, exacted some minor form of retribution on the *Orient Express*, with the destruction of carriage 2419 in 1944. A German panzer regiment had seized the car from the Compagnie's building where it was being showcased to the exact spot where the Armistice had been signed in 1918.

At first, Hitler used the car to dictate surrender terms to the French delegation. The car was then taken to Berlin and exhibited beside the Brandenburg Gate before being moved to a rail siding 180 miles from Berlin. Here the SS blew up the carriage and with it a significant piece of the train's history was obliterated.

However, with Hitler and Germany eventually defeated in 1945, the *Orient Express* was free again to resume service. This was not without its problems as the Iron Curtain drew a tight reign across parts of Europe and Communist nations insisted on using their own carriages to take over services at almost

every border.

The Cold War was becoming colder and the controls at every frontier were becoming increasingly severe. Even the French and Swiss examined the passports and baggage thoroughly.

Tension between Russia and the Allies grew after the breakdown of the Four Powers conference in December 1947 and within six months the Iron Curtain became almost impenetrable. However, that the trains continued to run at the height of the Cold War was testimony to the strict neutrality of the Compagnie's policy.

Few people, other than diplomats and Communist officials and officers of the armed forces of Russia and her Balkan satellites travelled on the eastern sections of the route. The attempt to maintain a regular schedule was partly for the sake of prestige but also in the hope that normal conditions (i.e. those up to 1939) would eventually be restored.

The Simplon *Orient Express* became very popular among the privileged who could obtain permits to travel, and its mouth-watering cuisine provided the Communist hierarchy with a taste of the luxurious living that even austerity-controlled Western Europe could provide as part of a normal service to travellers on its express trains.

The Arlberg *Orient Express* was always fully booked on its run through Austria, and protests of refusals of permits from the Soviet members were comparatively rare. The secret instructions sent down the line to guards at the checkpoints were, though, another matter. Every passenger had to have a grey pass in addition to his/her passport and travel permit. The grey pass was the target for the Soviet guards when they had instructions to harass passengers.

By 1961 the train was not running beyond Bucharest, and its restaurant cars only went as far as Vienna, where the majority of passengers alighted. However, improvements in the track in Romania and Bulgaria and the desire of the Balkan countries to have the benefits of this easily controlled means of communication with the West resulted in the train not only surviving what was described as its "final run" in 1961, but it slowly resumed its earlier routing as far as Istanbul, with a line to Athens.

For 10 years the train, though

Far Left: Iron Curtain States.

Centre: An *Orient Express* Pullman car.

considerably reduced in size, luxury and reliability ran from Paris to Istanbul and back. Passenger numbers travelling the whole distance were low but it was valuable for intermediate journeys. As such more stops were scheduled, linking the capitals of Austria, Hungary and the Balkans.

The fact that the Wagon–Lits trains continued to run virtually without final cancellation of any service was a testament to the diplomatic skills of the Compagnie in dealing with the railroads and governments of eight nations, some of whom had severed relationships with their neighbours. The Simplon *Orient Express* was still leaving dead on time and arriving with only occasional delays.

However, by 1972 the *Orient Express'* death warrant had been signed. By then it existed in name only. It was now a succession of separate trains to which the Wagon-Lits sleeping cars were coupled on and off. In 1974, the Thomas Cook Group terminated its representation of the sleeping services on the continent. The Nagelmackers Compagnie dropped from its title the proud term "Grands Express Europeens" and ominously added "du Tourisme".

LUXURY ON WHEELS

YOU TAKE YOUR HOTEL ALONG WITH YOU BY THIS ROUTE.

MEALS ENJOYED AT LEISURE

INTERIOR VIEW OF DINING CAR ON

CHICAGO & ALTON R. R. LINES

MEALS, 75 CENTS.

Far Left: The *Orient Express.*

Left: Pullman Car poster.

LITTLE BOOK OF THE **ORIENT EXPRESS**

The Direct-*Orient Express* made its last appearance along the track across Europe in May 1977, the end of a grand performance that had lasted for 94 years. A lot had changed in that time. The Austro-Hungarian, French, German and Italian empires had faded away. Many Emperors, rulers and dictators had risen and fallen. Nations had been broken up and new ones created.

The greatest change of them all was the invisible but all too real Iron Curtain. After an interminable series of arguments and negotiations, the *Orient Express* had eventually managed to penetrate it. It was, though, defenceless against the one form of transportation that proved to be its ultimate nemesis: the aeroplanes that cocked a snook at the train's 67-hour journey by completing theirs in less than three.

The last run was to leave Paris' Gare de Lyon at 11.53pm on 19 May 1977, commemorating the train's reputation by departing precisely on time. Unfortunately, due to a delay in coupling the locomotive, it didn't manage to stick to this tradition.

The train's old glories were conspicuous by their absence also. No opulent restaurant or sleeping cars. Only 18 passengers on this last *Orient Express* managed to get sleeping berths, most were press or TV reporters.

Despite the massive lack of luxury compared to the *Orient Express* of old, nothing could erase the glamour of the final journey for those on board. The usual inconvenient modern day border checks occasionally threatened to cast a pall over proceedings but these were miniscule issues on what was a largely smooth and memorable adventure.

When the train came to a final halt, 5 hours, 38 minutes behind schedule in Serketchi station in Istanbul, the delay had done nothing to dampen the mood of those passengers who had made the historic journey. Bottles of champagne were opened, *Auld Lang Syne* was sung – to the utter bewilderment of the staff.

On that May day in 1977, the *Orient Express* may have been relegated to history but the rails on which it ran still snaked their way across Europe, and the irrepressible reputation of the train and the tracks that existed for other luxury trains to embark on the same journey ensured that this was not the last the world was to see of this once great train.

In 1982 the *Orient Express* was established as a private venture and restored to its former glory as in the 1930s. Until its closure in 2007, the train had catered for passengers paying more than £1,000 each to travel between London, Paris and Venice on a weekly basis.

Throughout the history of the *Orient Express* there have many different routes but sadly the route was discontinued from the summer of 2007 when the TGV – *train à grande vitesse* or high speed train – took over the direct rail line which was built direct to Istanbul in 1889.

In North America, the American *Orient Express*, formerly the American European Express, operated several train sets in charter service between 1989 and 2008.

On 12 December 2009, the *Orient Express* ceased to operate and the route disappeared from European railway timetables, reportedly a 'victim of high-speed trains and cut-rate airlines'. The Venice-Simplon *Orient Express* train, a private venture by Orient-Express Hotels using original carriages from the 1920s and 30s, continues to run from London to Venice and to other destinations in Europe, including the original route from Paris to Istanbul.

The legendary Venice-Simplon Orient-Express is poised to embark on a series of exciting new rail voyages to Scandinavia in April 2013.

A scenic two-night journey will take it from Venice to Stockholm, via an overnight stop in Copenhagen. Its return journey, four days later, will depart Stockholm, via Copenhagen, for Venice. This new route will mark the first occasion in the train's long history that it has visited Stockholm.

For centuries, man had to be content with the horse as a means of transport – if he could afford it. If not it was a case of making do on foot. Then, all of a sudden, the bicycle, internal combustion engine, aeroplane and helicopter arrived. And now, with modern day's congested roads taking the fun out of travel, we search for different means of medium range transport, which leaves rail travel as still the most majestic way to travel.

You sit back in your comfortable seat, as if sat in your very own limousine, watching life go by as you travel to your destination. And the pinnacle of such a way to travel was the *Orient Express*.

Left: Copenhagen route.

London

Ostende

Dover

Calais

Brüssel

Köln

Amiens

Frankfurt am Main

Kurswagen Ostende-Wien-Orient-Express (ab 1900)

Berlin

Frankfurt an der Oder

Nürnberg

Paris

Châlons-sur-Marne
Châlons-en-Champagne

Stuttgart

Nancy

Straßburg

Simbach

Pas

bis 1897

München

ab 1897

Salzbu

Züge nac

Orient-Express 1883-1914

Grenzen: 1914

▬▬▬▬ Orient - Express (O.E.)
▬▬▬▬ Hauptzug / Kurswagen

▬▬▬▬ Zubringerzug
- - - - Schiffsverbindung

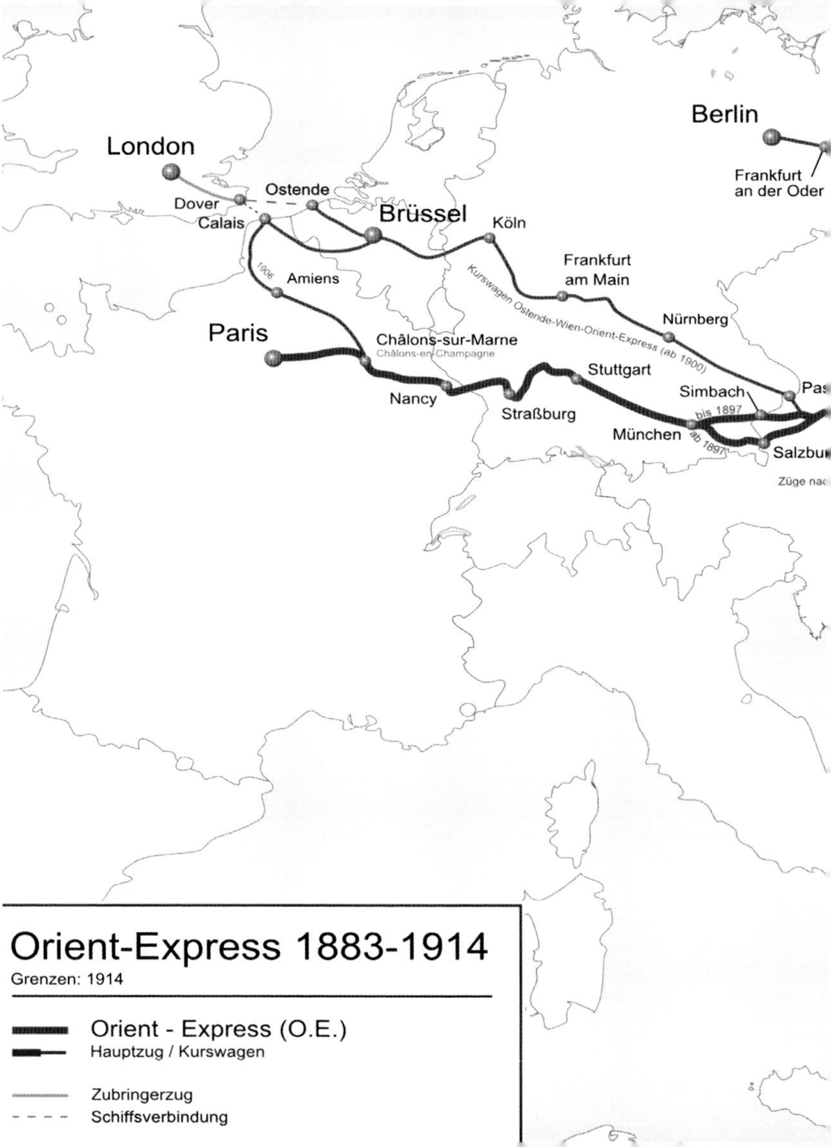

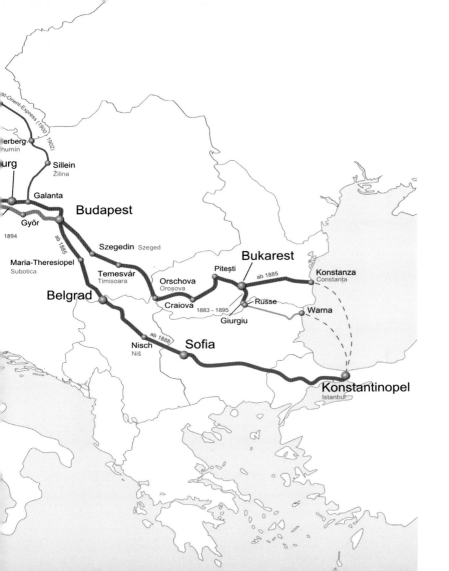

st-Orient-Express (1900/1902)

erberg
humin

urg

Sillein
Žilina

Galanta

Budapest

Györ

1894

ab 1885

Szegedin   Szeged

Maria-Theresiopel
Subotica

Temesvár
Timisoara

Bukarest

Piteşti

Konstanza
Constanţa

Orschova
Oroşova

ab 1885

Belgrad

Craiova

1883 - 1895

Russe

Warna

Giurgiu

Nisch
Niš

ab 1888

Sofia

Konstantinopel
Istanbul

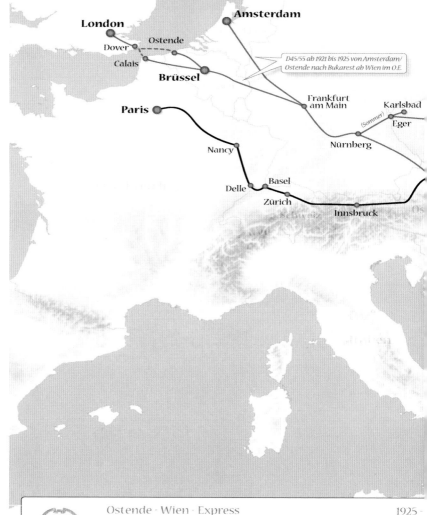

Centre: *Orient Express* 1919 - 1939 route.

D45/55 ab 1921 bis 1925 von Amsterdam/ Ostende nach Bukarest ab Wien im O.E.

London

Amsterdam

Dover

Ostende

Calais

Brüssel

Frankfurt am Main

Karlsbad

(Sommer)

Eger

Paris

Nürnberg

Nancy

Delle

Basel

Zürich

Innsbruck

Schweiz

Ostende - Wien - Express   1925 -

Suisse - Arlberg - Vienne - Express (S.A.V.E.)   1925 -

(ab 1930 als Arlberg - Orent -Express unterwegs bis Budapest)

O.W.O.E. & S.A.V.E.

1919 - 1939
Grenzen: 1937

Bratislava

Budapest

Cegled

Oradea

Wien - Bukarest ab 1927 als D-Zug

Cluj-Napoca

Sighişoara

Pitesti

Bukarest

Belgrad

Paris- Athen 1930 - 1939 ab Belgrad im Simplon - Orient - Express

Niš

Sofia

Thessaloniki

Istanbul

Athen

The History of Luxury Train Travel

Today there is a marked increase in the trend of luxury train travel around the world, and the reason for this is that this form of transportation boasts several distinct advantages over travelling on airplanes.

Whereas during air travel the monotony of the journey is occasionally broken by the view of the clouds through the plane's window, a winding luxury ride on board a train provides ample opportunity to the guests to witness the plethora of colours of the places they are travelling to.

There are a number of reasons for the growing popularity of the luxury trains over air travel, which include ample space, restaurants and bars, spacious and comfortable sleeping and seating area and even wash/bathrooms. Since the time of introduction of *Pioneer* in 1864 by American industrialist George Mortimer Pullman, luxury train travel has come a long way, and despite the *Orient Express* being the most famous, there have been many other lauded trains and routes.

World Famous Trains and Routes

The Flying Scotsman

Between London's King's Cross station and Edinburgh Waverley is 390 miles of East Coast Main Line that the *Flying Scotsman*, possibly one of the most famous steam trains in the world, used to regularly travel up and down.

The line itself was built by three companies during the Victorian period with the first section between London and Doncaster having been constructed by Great Northern Railway. Work was finished in 1853, however, it took the North Eastern Railway another 23 years to build and finish the next stretch of line between Doncaster and Berwick.

The *Flying Scotsman* became accessible to the wider public when third–class tickets were introduced in 1888.

The final section of the line was finished first by the North British Railway from Berwick to Edinburgh in 1846. A terminus was built at York within the city walls and trains, whether travelling north or south, were required to reverse into the original station. A new station alleviated the problem in 1877; however, trains were faced with the same issue at Newcastle station as the site in the city was also built as a terminus.

The problem was solved with the King Edward VII Bridge built in 1906. The line remained pretty much as it was built originally except when a 13-mile diversion to avoid subsidence over an active mining area was constructed around Selby coalfield in 1983.

Service began for this famous train in 1923. The official name of the *Flying Scotsman* was originally the *Special Scotch Express*, which ran exclusively for first- and second-class ticket holders at 10am each day. The journey was incredibly long at more than 10 hours, although lunch was served in York and passengers had 30 minutes to stretch their legs.

The train had rival companies wanting to offer a faster service than the famous locomotive and the *Flying Scotsman* ended up reducing its journey time to eight and a half hours when it ran non-stop.

After 1924, the train's name was changed from the *Special Scotch Express*, and the *Flying Scotsman* was born, as was the non-stop service between London and Edinburgh in 1928.

In a response to the decline of steam, the train journey was again reduced between 1932 and 1938 but the Second World War brought changes and

overcrowding was common. Despite the speed of the HSTs, the National Railway Museum was hoping to re-licence the *Flying Scotsman* during 2007 so that it would once more grace the East Coast Main Line.

From 23 May 2011 the *Flying Scotsman* brand was relaunched for a special, daily, fast service operated by East Coast departing Edinburgh at 05.40 and reaching London in exactly four hours, calling only at Newcastle. It is operated by an InterCity 225 'Mallard' set. Class 91 locomotive 91101 was turned out in a special *Flying Scotsman* livery for the opening day of the service.

East Coast claims that this is part of a policy to bring back named trains to restore 'a touch of glamour and romance'. However, for the first time in its history, it runs in one direction only: there is no northbound equivalent service. Northbound, the fastest timetabled London-to-Edinburgh service now takes 4 hours 19 minutes.

Despite the high-speed trains of today, the *Flying Scotsman* is still the most talked about train on the East Coast Main Line and all modern trains sport the words "The route of the Flying Scotsman" on their engines.

Far Left: The *Flying Scotsman* approaches Clapham station.

The Glacier Express

Left: The *Glacier Express*.

To travel from Zermatt in Switzerland to St Moritz on a seven and a half hour journey there is only one route to take – the *Glacier Express*. Alternatively, passengers can take the train from Piz Bernina to the Matterhorn which crosses 291 bridges and steams through 91 tunnels before crossing the Oberalp Pass at more than 6,562 feet above sea level.

This stunning panoramic journey through the Swiss Alps is simply breathtaking and passengers can enjoy views of central Switzerland, the Graubünden region, Lake Lucerne and Lucerne. The *Glacier Express* also passes through the Valais region with its glaciers and the mountain forests as well as meandering alongside Alpine meadows, mountain streams and valleys.

Those with the resources to travel on the *Glacier Express* were regular visitors in the 1920s who brought about the transformation of Zermatt and St Moritz from sleepy, remote villages into up and coming resorts. During the 1920s, there were three railway companies in the

region including VZ (later BVZ), RhB and FOB.

All three railways realised the potential of the tourist industry and in 1926 the route between Valais and Graubünden was opened. Despite the relative advances of the day it was to take another 50 years before it was possible to travel through the Furka region during the cold, winter months. In 1930, the Visp to Brig route was opened and the train made its inaugural journey between Zermatt and St Moritz.

Two companies VZ and RhB were equipped with electric engines, however steam was the only mode of travel with FOB. The steam locomotives were eventually sent to Vietnam in the mid-1940s but returned home five decades later and have been providing today's passengers with nostalgic train rides since the early 1990s. Also during the 1940s, due to the unsettled environment as a result of the Second World War, services were scaled down and were only reintroduced in 1948 where changes were evident.

The following two decades brought developments, and faster engines were brought in to cut costs and bring down travelling times – as was happening across Europe, the UK and the US. It was during the 1970s that work was carried out on the Furka Alpine route to ensure that the line was safe through the winter months. The route was finally ready for all-year travel in 1982.

The 1980s and 1990s proved to be a boom time for the *Glacier Express* and tourists flocked to ride on the famous train in their droves. In June 2005, the *Glacier Express* celebrated 75 years of service and is a tourist attraction that the Swiss are as proud of today as they were more than seven decades ago.

Rocky Mountaineer

In 1990, Canada's national rail operator Via Rail sold off its "Rockies by daylight" scenic train to a private company called Rocky Mountaineer Vacations based in Vancouver, who renamed it the *Rocky Mountaineer.* Featured on the BBC's list of *50 Things to do Before You Die*, Rocky Mountaineer Rail takes the guest on a once-in-a-lifetime tour along the Rocky Mountains with its snow covered peaks, huge forests and glacier-fed lakes in Canada.

It is the busiest privately-owned passenger rail service in North America, having transported over one million passengers since 1990, and operates on four different routes in the Canadian Rockies, through spectacular scenery with truly world class service on board:

- Over the Canadian Pacific Railway (CP) on the *First Passage to the West* route from Vancouver, British Columbia via Kamloops to Banff or Calgary, Alberta.

- Over the Canadian National Railway (CN) on the *Journey through the Clouds* route from Vancouver via Kamloops to Jasper, Alberta.

- The *Rainforest to Gold Rush* route over the CN operated portion from North Vancouver via Whistler and Quesnel through Prince George to Jasper.

- The *Whistler Sea to Sky Climb* return day-trip from North Vancouver to Whistler.

The *First Passage to the West* and *Journey through the Clouds* route trains depart from *Rocky Mountaineer*'s station at 1755 Cottrell Street just off Terminal Avenue in Vancouver. The *Whistler Sea to Sky Climb* route trains depart from a platform at the corner of Philip Avenue and West 1st Street in North Vancouver. The *Whistler Sea to* Sky Climb route connects to the Rainforest to Gold Rush route, which departs from *Rocky Mountaineer*'s platform at the Nita Lake Lodge in the Creekside area of Whistler.

Rocky Mountaineer was awarded the "World's Leading Travel Experience by Train" in 2005, 2006 and 2007 at the World Travel Awards, has been listed among the World's Top 25 Trains since 2005 by The Society of International Railway Travelers, and was recognised by *National Geographic Magazine* as one of the "World's Best Journeys" in 2007. The Society of American Travel Writers, the world's largest organisation of professional travel journalists and photographers, rated the *Rocky Mountaineer* as the world's top train ride in 2009.

Hiram Bingham

Providers of luxury train tours in Peru, Hiram Bingham is part of the luxury *Orient Express* service. This train charts the course of scenic Machu Picchu, a designated UNESCO World Heritage Site.

Northern Belle

Owned by Venice-Simplon *Orient Express*, *Northern Belle* is a luxury train operating rail tours and charters that complement the programme of the *British Pullman* train. Introduced in 2000, the train consists primarily of British Rail Mark 2 coaching stock, refurbished internally and painted externally to resemble the vintage *Brighton Belle* coaches of the *British Pullman*.

The buffet cars are British Rail Mark 1 coaches. Unlike the *British Pullman*, the train primarily operates in the north of England and Scotland. The train also has two British Rail Mark 3 sleeper coaches for its crew.

The train embarks from a number of Northern UK cities, including Liverpool, Edinburgh, Glasgow and Manchester. *Northern Belle* comprises six dining cars named after historic British houses.

Eastern and Oriental Express

The exclusive *Eastern and Oriental Express*, winding through some of the most exotic and spectacular locales from Bangkok to Singapore via Kuala Lumpur, offers an unforgettable ride through mystic landscapes. Covering more than 1,243 miles of peninsular South East Asia, the two-day journey offered by the *Eastern and*

Oriental Express has frequent stops at scenic locations.

This luxury train has three classes of coach, elegant décor and comes equipped with contemporary amenities, including 24-hour steward service, international electric sockets (220 volts) and a 110 volt adapter for razors, a personal safe and hairdryer. All coaches are fully air-conditioned and come with en suite shower and washbasin. *Eastern and Oriental Express* offers four distinct journeys, which lets you discover the mystique and enchantment of peninsular Asia.

British Pullman

The *British Pullman* train takes its name from George Mortimer Pullman, founder of the Pullman Car Company. One of the key attributes which sets the *British Pullman* train apart is that it consists of the vintage carriages which ran on the legendary 1920s services of the original *Orient Express*. The *British Pullman* train can carry 226 passengers and comes with a total of 11 carriages, which bear testimony to the history and legend that is *Orient Express*.

Quaint décor, exquisite artistic skills, art deco marquetry along with consummate hospitality gives an unmatchable character to this luxury train. Each carriage of this train is a walking gallery of grandeur.

Each name has its own history, its own motif and its own legend. The guests on board the *British Pullman* train are offered gourmet dining options and each course is accompanied by rare wines and finest champagnes. The *British Pullman* train is arguably the best way to discover the British countryside.

Rovos Rail

Rovos Rail is a private railway company operating out of Capital Park Station in Pretoria, South Africa. Established in 1989, Rovos Rail is a luxury train in Africa that began its maiden journey on 29 April of the same year.

The Society of International Railway Travelers has regularly named the *Pride of Africa*, as the train is called, as one of the World's Top 25 Trains because of its excellent accommodation, public spaces, service, dining and off-train sightseeing.

Rovos Rail offers pan-African luxury train journeys spanning more than 24 hours to a fortnight. Rovos Rail also offers private rail charters, golf tours and a special journey

Far Left: A British Pullman train at Bristol Temple Meads.

spanning more than seven African countries combining Rovos Rail, private plane and a five-star luxury cruise.

Palace on Wheels

*P*alace on Wheels, voted as the fourth best luxury train in the world is a luxury train in India, offering guests a luxurious ride across destinations in Rajasthan along with Agra.

The train's first journey was on 26 January, India's Republic Day, in 1982 and the train boasted 14 coaches named after the princely states of erstwhile Rajputana. The aesthetics and décor of the salons reflect the heritage, culture and opulence of the Maharajas of the bygone era. The train also houses two pantry cars, a bar and a lounge for the pleasure of the guests.

Operated by Rajasthan Tourism Development Corporation Ltd., a government of Rajasthan undertaking, the train departs from New Delhi and during its eight-day journey, travels around Rajasthan with stops in Jaipur, Jaisalmer, Jodhpur, Sawai Madhopur, Chittaurgarh, Udaipur, Bharatpur and Agra.

Earlier, tickets for the *Palace on Wheels* were restricted to foreign nationals only by the Government of India, with Indian natives not allowed on board. However, it was later opened up to Indians as well, although even today tariffs are quoted in US dollars.

Maharajas Express

The *Maharajas Express* is a luxury train in India, billed as the country's answer to the *Orient Express* and is owned by the Indian Railways Catering and Tourism Corporation. This luxurious train service was started in March 2010, when the Indian Railway Catering and Tourism Corporation Limited (IRCTC) and Cox and Kings India Ltd. signed a joint venture to set up a company called Royale Indian Rail Tours Ltd. (RIRTL) to oversee the functioning and management of the *Maharajas Express*. However, this joint venture was terminated on 12 August 2011 and the train is now being operated exclusively by IRCTC.

The *Maharajas Express* is the most expensive luxury train in India and in 2011 it was named in the 2011 list of World's Top 25 Trains by The Society of

International Railway Travelers.

The train comprises 23 carriages, which include accommodation, dining, bar, lounge, generator and store cars. Accommodation is available in 14 guest carriages with a total passenger capacity of 88. The accommodations on board are categorised as Deluxe cabins, Junior Suites, Suites and a Grand Presidential Suite that spans an entire carriage. Each guest carriage has been designed to recreate the opulence of Maharaja-style living.

The train also has a lounge called the Rajah Club with a private bar, two dining cars and a dedicated bar car, while an onboard souvenir boutique offers memorabilia for passengers. The train is also equipped with a water filtration plant.

Royal Rajasthan on Wheels

This Indian luxury train commenced its service from December 2009. *Royal Rajasthan on Wheels* was launched on the queue of *Palace on Wheels* (RRoW), the most revered and popular luxury train in India. The train takes the guests on a regal ride of destinations in Rajasthan, and recently two destinations, Khajuraho and Varanasi, were added to the itinerary of the train.

This train, composed of 22 coaches, can carry 82 passengers in a journey with one Super Deluxe saloon, 13 Deluxe Saloons and two restro-lounges. With facilities like spa and fitness centre on board, *Royal Rajasthan on Wheels* is one of the most luxurious trains in the world.

Blue Train

Blue Train combines the best of a luxury five-star hotel's interiors and the irresistible allure of leisure train travel across several destinations in South Africa. Its origins date back to the *Union Limited* and *Union Express* trains which began in 1923, taking passengers from Johannesburg to the ships departing from Cape Town to England. The *Union Express* introduced luxury features such as a dining saloon in 1933 and air-conditioned carriages in 1939.

After a break in service in the Second World War, the service returned in 1946. With the reintroduction of the train, the colloquial "blue train" moniker, a reference to the blue-painted steel carriages

THE HISTORY OF LUXURY TRAIN TRAVEL

Right: The *Blue Train.*

LITTLE BOOK OF THE **ORIENT EXPRESS**

introduced in 1937, was formally adopted as the new name.

In 1997 it was refurbished and relaunched and has gone on to win the prestigious Africa's Leading Luxury Train award for two years in a row (2009 and 2010).

Prior to 2002, the *Blue Train* operated on four distinct routes:

- the main Pretoria–Cape Town service

- the scenic "Garden Route" from Cape Town to Port Elizabeth

- to Hoedspruit, along the western edge of Kruger Park

- to Zimbabwe's Victoria Falls

By 2004 the last two routes had been suspended, the former due to lack of patronage, the latter due to erratic rail rates being charged for access to the network of financially strapped Zimbabwe. As of 2007, the only regular route in operation was Pretoria–Cape Town, however, special package tours are available to Durban or the Bakubung Game Lodge. This train is also available for private charter.

The Golden Chariot

The *Golden Chariot* is a luxury tourist train that connects the important tourist spots in the Indian states of Karnataka and Goa. It is named after the Stone Chariot in the Vitthala Temple at Hampi. The 19 coaches on the train are coloured purple and gold, and sport the logo of a mythological animal with the head of an elephant and a body of a lion. The *Golden Chariot* operates weekly and had its maiden commercial run on 10 March 2008.

The train, along with the *Deccan Odyssey*, is designed on the lines of the more popular *Palace on Wheels* with accommodations, spa treatments and dining. The train is operated by the Karnataka State Tourism Development Corporation and marketed by The Luxury Trains, whereas The Mapple Group handles the hospitality services on the train.

Karnataka's luxury train, the *Golden Chariot*, ran with full occupancy for the first time since its launch four years ago, when it chugged out of Bangalore on 6 January 2012 for its 'Pride of the South' run across Karnataka and Goa.

The train offers a seven-day/eight-night tour of Bangalore, Kabini, Mysore, Hassan, Hospet, Badami and Goa, before returning to Bangalore. The tourist attractions visited include the Nagarhole National Park, Mysore Palace, Srirangapatna forts, Hoysaleswara Temple, Gomateshwara and the Badami Cave Temples. Passengers have the option to start their trips from either Bangalore or Goa.

The *Golden Chariot* also offers an extended two-week tour that covers Coimbatore, Madurai, Kanyakumari, Trivandrum, and Kochi during the second week.

The *Golden Chariot* offers accommodation in 44 cabins in 11 coaches that are named after dynasties that ruled the region: Kadamba, Hoysala, Rashtrakuta, Ganga, Chalukya, Bahamani, Adil Shahi, Sangama, Satavahana, Yadukula and Vijayanagar. It also has two restaurants, a lounge bar, and conference, gym and spa facilities. It is the only train in India to have onboard Wi-Fi connectivity, and satellite antennae providing live television service in the cabins.

The Ghan

Operated by Great Southern Railway Ltd, the *Ghan*, a luxury train in Australia, connects 1,851 miles of breathtaking locales through the heart of the Australian continent, from Darwin in the north to Adelaide in the south, on a twice-weekly service. Unfortunately, the current world financial crisis has reduced the frequency to one service a week during the low season (November to March).

In addition to Adelaide, Alice Springs, and Darwin, the train also makes a stop at Katherine. The stops at Katherine and Alice Springs allow time for optional tours. The average length of the train is 2,250 feet, but trains up to 49 carriages long (3,937 feet in length) have been run.

The service's name is an abbreviated version of its previous nickname, *The Afghan Express*, unofficially bestowed on the "express passenger" service of the Commonwealth Railways in 1923, by one of its crews. The train's name honours Afghan camel drivers who arrived in Australia in the late nineteenth century to help find a way to reach the country's unexplored interior.

Construction of what was then known as the Port Augusta to Government Gums Railway began in 1878 when the Premier of South Australia, Sir William Jervois,

broke ground at Port Augusta. The Cape gauge line reached Hawker in June 1880, Beltana in July 1881, Marree in January 1884 and Oodnadatta on 7 January 1891. It was not until 1926 that development to Alice Springs began, and that section was completed in 1929. Until then, the final leg of the train journey was still made by camel.

While there were plans from the beginning to extend the line through to Darwin, by the time the Alice Springs connection was complete, the *Ghan* was running at a financial loss, and plans for connection to Darwin were put on indefinite hold.

The original *Ghan* line followed the same track as the overland telegraph, which is believed to be the route taken by John McDouall Stuart during his 1862 crossing of Australia. It was notorious for washouts and other delays on the line, and the flatcar immediately behind the tender carried spare sleepers and railway tools, so that if a washout was encountered the passengers and crew could work as a railway gang to repair the line and permit the train to continue.

This appalling service was tolerated because steam trains needed water, and Stuart's route to Alice Springs was the only one that had available water.

During the Second World War, the service enjoyed a massive expansion, putting pressure on the limited water supplies. Consequently, demineralisation towers were built along the track so that bore water could be used, some of which survive to this day. When steam was replaced by diesel there was no need for water, and the line was rerouted to the waterless (but more reliable) route from Tarcoola to Alice Springs.

The original *Ghan* ran for the last time in 1980 and today The Ghan Preservation Society is principled with its preservation and upkeep. It was not until October 1980 that a new standard gauge line from Tarcoola, South Australia (a siding on the Trans-Australian Railway) to Alice Springs was constructed, and the train took the form it has today. The new line is located approximately 99 miles west of the former line, in an effort to prevent washout due to rain and improve the train's performance.

The new Ghan line

Construction of the Alice Springs-Darwin line was believed to be the second-largest civil engineering project in Australia, and the largest in the 50 years since the creation of the Snowy Mountains Scheme (built 1949–1974). Line construction began in July 2001, with the first passenger train reaching Darwin on 4 February 2004, after 126 years of planning and waiting and at a cost of A$1.3 billion.

The *Ghan*'s arrival in Darwin signified a new era of tourism in the Northern Territory, making travel to the region easier and more convenient as well as providing better access to and for Aboriginal communities in the region, and allowing for more freight to travel through the region.

Golden Eagle Trans-Siberian Express

Dubbed the journey of a lifetime by many who have experienced it, the iconic *Trans-Siberian Railway* offers passengers the chance to travel across nine countries and nine different time zones on a 13-day excursion that travels the same distance as crossing the United States three times.

The route connects Moscow and Eurasia with the far east of Russia, Mongolia, China and the Sea of Japan. With its main route running from Moscow to Vladivostok via Siberia, the *Trans-Siberian Railway* is steeped in history that dates back to 1891, when work on the railway began.

Finished 25 years later, the route is in excess of 5,770 miles and is the third-longest single, continuous service across the globe. There are four main routes on the railway where the last, which runs further north than the others, was introduced as recently as 1991.

Siberia was decidedly undeveloped at the end of the 1800s partly due to a lack of transportation systems. Roads were few and rivers were the only real means of transportation – either by boat during the warmer months, or by a horse-drawn sled when the rivers had iced over during the harsh winter months.

Encouraged by the Moscow/ St Petersburg Railway, efforts were made to encourage industry and the building of the railway in Siberia. By 1880 there were a number of applications that had been submitted and rejected and the design process took an entire decade to complete. Some suggestions included using ferries rather than bridges for crossing rivers but

THE HISTORY OF LUXURY TRAIN TRAVEL

the architects succeeded in having plans for a continuous railway agreed. Sergei Witte, the then finance minister was responsible for overseeing the building of the project while engineers began work on both ends of the line.

By 1898 construction – undertaken by convicts and Russian soldiers – had reached Lake Baikal (the largest, deepest and oldest lake in the world). The railway ended each side of the lake and an icebreaker ferry was bought to connect the two lines.

The coming of the railway gave Siberia a tremendous boost in agriculture enabling exports to central Russia and Europe. The *Trans-Siberian Railway* still remains a vital link in Russia's transportation services and around 30 per cent of exports are still carried by train. Domestically it is also a crucial link for local passengers, as well as the huge array of tourists from across the globe.

The *Golden Eagle Trans-Siberian Express* launched in April 2007 takes the guests on a luxurious 6,000-mile adventure, the world's longest train journey, across two continents and eight time zones. It traverses the course of the famous Trans-Siberian Railroad which connects Moscow and European Russia with the Russian Far East provinces, Mongolia, China and the Sea of Japan.

The Rich,
The Renowned
and The Royals

Far Right:
Herbert Hoover.

During its long and illustrious existence, the *Orient Express* must have carried hundreds of thousands of passengers and its archives still preserve many of the booking lists, some of which read like pages from the *International Who's Who*.

Luminaries who travelled on board include figures such as Haile Selassie, on his way to his London exile after Mussolini's army had overrun his country; Cardinal Pacelli – later Pope Pius XII – on a tour of Europe; Sir Maurice Hankey, the powerful decision maker behind six British cabinets; Theodor Herzl, the founder of Zionism, and Chaim Weizmann, the future President of the State of Israel.

Before the start of the First World War, a young American engineer called Herbert Hoover was a frequent passenger, surveying proposed oil fields, while after the war, the famous novelist F. Scott Fitzgerald was also seen on board.

World-famous stars

Among this impressive and long list resided one of the most famous early passengers, the French stage actress Sarah Bernhardt, regarded by many as the greatest actress of the

Above: The world-renowned composer Arturo Toscanini.

music, from Gustav Mahler, Hans von Bulow, Max Bruch, even Debussy to Mascagni and in a later era, Richard Strauss. However, among the famous conductors, the most frequent passenger was Arturo Toscanini, who raised his baton in concert halls the world over, and was most famously the musical director of Milan's La Scala.

And then there is the equally impressive array of royal figures that travelled on the train. The earliest patron was, of course, Belgium's King Leopold II, Georges Nagelmackers' chief subscriber. Leopold was notorious for his incredible frugality. He wore the same shirt for days on end and rarely tipped his attendants; if he did it was with small coins.

century, Maurice Chevalier, Ernest Hemingway and the iconic Marlene Dietrich. However, the number of famous stars of the world of music and ballet far eclipsed that of the theatre and silver screen. It appeared that every great conductor, concert virtuoso or prima donna and ballerina had at one time travelled on the train.

The names read like a dictionary of

British royalty

While Queen Victoria did not travel, due to the fact that she had her own royal train, her son Edward VII, when he was Prince of Wales, did travel on the *Orient Express*. Edward made use of Europe's most lavish train when making many discreet trips to Paris, the

South of France and Central Europe, invariably in the company of beautiful women and under the pseudonym, "the Duke of Lancaster". Usually one of his salon cars was attached to the regularly scheduled express.

The Duke of York – later, King George VI – attended, in Belgrade in 1922, the marriage of King Alexander of Yugoslavia to Princess Marie of Romania and the *Orient Express* was his home for the entire route. As it was when the train again carried the newly married Prince to Belgrade for the christening of Crown Prince Peter.

However, the most regular *Orient Express* passenger among British royalty was Edward VIII, who later became the Duke of Windsor. Before he met his future wife Wallis Simpson, Edward, as Prince of Wales, made frequent trips between London, Paris and Vienna. The trips were explained as necessary for consulting a famous Austrian physician who treated him for a chronic ear problem. But the prince combined them with social distractions with his friends.

Once he had controversially married Mrs Simpson and abdicated his throne on 11 December 1936, the ex-King (no longer having to travel incognito)

Above: Haile Selassie.

took the *Orient Express* to Vienna. This journey, conducted as to ensure Edward escaped the attention of newspaper reporters, was extremely different to the one that he had enjoyed only six months previously, when he was King. He was still in a first-class compartment but this time the meals were served on trays that were balanced on top of two suitcases spread over the gap of the seats.

Right: Wallis
Simpson in 1936.

Six months later the Duke of Windsor and Mrs Simpson returned by *Orient Express* to France, where they were married at the Chateau de Conde near Tours.

European royalty

A ccustomed as royal travellers were to treating the *Orient Express* as their own personal means of transportation, their occasional inconsiderate demands and interference with the running of the train had to be endured by the Compagnie and its staff.

After all, the royals provided a lucrative source of revenue and the prestige they bestowed on the Wagon-Lits was invaluable. The worst offenders by far were the Balkan rulers, whose every wish had to be fulfilled. Unfortunately, some of the Balkan kings could claim that but for their cooperation there would have been no properly maintained railroad for the expresses to run on, or even no track at all.

Innumerable trips on the *Orient Express* took Ferdinand I of Bulgaria around Europe. Ferdinand, as the youngest son of Prince Augustus of Saxe-Coburg and Princess Clementine of Bourbon-Orleans, was extremely suitable to be put on any vacant throne where Queen Victoria and Germany's Bismarck each considered it of potential value.

However, Ferdinand was quite the astute statesman and he played politicians and army generals off against one another, securing his position internally. This policy also served him well on the international front and on his subsequent travels on board the train he visited the Sultan of Turkey, the Emperor of Austro-Hungary, the German Kaiser and the King of Greece, amongst others.

But the comfort of his special salon car (which he had demanded to be attached to the train when he made one of his international trips) was not enough. He liked to drive the train. Fortunately, after an early mishap when he had taken control of the train, he only took over at scheduled stops.

And it wasn't just Ferdinand who liked to drive the *Orient Express*; in later years his son Boris developed the same penchant as his father, and again was rather good at doing so. Unfortunately, the outbreak of the Second World War put paid to any further train driving by

THE RICH, THE RENOWNED AND THE ROYALS

Right: King Carol II of Romania - one of the most unpredictable royal figures who graced the train.

LITTLE BOOK OF THE **ORIENT EXPRESS**

Boris (by now the King).

He did not survive the war, his death, at the age of 49, was never fully explained. However, there was little doubt that he had been poisoned by Gestapo agents in conspiracy with pro-Nazi officers of his palace guards, after Boris had secretly tried to contact the Allies in the hope of resisting the growing Nazi oppression. Unfortunately, his double dealing was discovered by Hitler's military intelligence.

Carol II of Romania

One of the last, and perhaps the most unpredictable, of the European royal devotees of the *Orient Express* was Romania's Carol II.

By the age of four he had already enjoyed regular journeys on the train, making regular journeys with his mother for vacations in England and on the French Riviera. Carol had always made a habit out of making the headlines and the train was the host for his final bizarre adventure.

Carol was a ruthless man, who had,

in 1933, issued his second wife with an ultimatum that she go into exile or never again be able to see their son Michael. Reluctantly agreeing, Queen Helen boarded the *Orient Express* bound for Paris at Bucharest station.

By early 1938, Carol was ostensibly the dictator of Romania, and believed himself to have absolute power over the army, police and parliament. And so he telephoned his long-term mistress Magda and told her it was finally safe to return to the country after a lengthy exile for fear of Carol losing his grasp on the crown. However, in the summer of 1940 Hitler and Stalin grabbed whatever Romanian territory they needed, and on 6 September Carol was forced to abdicate and leave his country.

He boarded the *Orient Express* just after midnight on 8 September, his contents including El Greco masterpieces removed from the palace walls, a vast stamp collection, dozens of first editions of books and cases of money.

The journey was uneventful until the train passed near Timisoara. Gun flashes in the darkness spurted out from both sides. Carol dragged his mistress along the floor to the bathroom, where he thrust her into the bath, holding her down with his own body. The *Orient Express* sped on and reached the safety of neutral Switzerland the following morning.

Carol would never travel on the *Orient Express* again. He finally married his mistress in 1947 in Brazil, and his now wife, one of the twentieth century's most notorious women went on to survive him by 24 years.

Paul Deschanel

The train's special PR trains (the initials stood for President de la Republique) first used by Czar Nicholas II for a state visit to Paris, were subsequently used by the Presidents of the Republic and were known as L'Elysee sur Rail. The most enthusiastic user was Raymond Poincare, who was president throughout the First World War. But it was his successor Paul Deschanel, who was the victim of one of the most bizarre mishaps ever recorded on the Wagon-Lits.

On 23 May 1920, he left Paris on the presidential train to unveil a monument at Montbrison, near Lyons. However, while an early breakfast was served the following morning the *chef de train* was counting the passengers as a railroad telegraph had informed him that someone had fallen out of the train 20 miles back.

No one was worried when all but the President were accounted for, but upon checking his sleeping car the alarming truth became known: his was the body seen falling from the speeding train. Fortunately, Deschanel, bruised and shivering in his pyjamas, had managed to reach the hut of a level-crossing keeper. It took some time for him to convince the man of his true identity and not some lunatic.

A belated official bulletin explained to an intrigued nation that the President, feeling unwell, had left his sleeping car and tried to open a window to get some fresh air. By mistake he opened a door and fell headlong, fortunately unharmed.

Inevitable rumours began to fly around. Was he drunk? Was he mentally unhinged? Had he been the victim of an attempted assassination? Either way, satirical journals had a field day. Deschanel endured the aspersions cast on his character and mental state for four months and then he resigned.

Basil Zaharoff – The Train's Ultimate VIP

For every Marlene Dietrich and Gloria Swanson on board the *Orient Express* there were many other shadowy, unknown figures travelling that were far wealthier. One such person was Basil Zaharoff, a man who, out of all the rich and influential people to travel on the *Orient Express*, would become the most frequent user of all.

Zaharoff was a Turkish businessman who traded in arms and weaponry. He got his start at the age of 22 selling submarines to anyone who had the financial means to do so. From the Greeks to the Turks, he sold his submarines without compunction for how they were subsequently to be used.

Zaharoff gave new meaning to unparalleled power and wealth, and like many mad emperors before him, Zaharoff put himself above morality; the only difference between him and these emperors was that he was completely sane.

By the inception of the First World War, there wasn't a submarine in the world in which Zaharoff hadn't been part of the transaction – and most of these transactions took place on board the *Orient Express*.

In an age when the railroad provided the sole means of relatively quick transport over long distances, the *Orient Express* became his temporary home. From the moment he made

Left: Boris Zaharoff.

BORIS ZAHAROFF - THE TRAIN'S ULTIMATE VIP

his inaugural journey on the *Orient Express* in 1885, he virtually lived on the train – it was his office, library and bedroom, and it played many roles in his fantastic career of ruthless intrigue, fortune hunting, bribery, and corruption – plus one incredible incident of romantic melodrama.

Zaharoff held a magnetic power over women. Wives and mistresses of ministers were wooed and rewarded for their infidelities with cash. They were also persuaded to divulge the secret weaknesses of their husbands and lovers. The girls were generously treated and sent back to a first-class sleeper which, however, was never to be compartment number seven.

But on one particular night on board the train, Zaharoff's life was to change immeasurably. As the train reached the vicinity of Salzburg, a loud, piercing scream rang out along the corridor. Zaharoff took little notice but was reassured by the sound of his personal bodyguard checking what was happening in the corridor. It was deserted.

He had hardly settled down when there was high-pitched agitated voice outside his compartment. Before

he could reach the door, there was a loud knocking and just as he slid the bolt on the door, it flew open to reveal a beautiful young woman who was semi-naked and sporting a deep scratch on her throat. Zaharoff's bodyguard came bursting into the compartment but to his surprise, his usually indignant master waved him away.

The girl suddenly shouted: 'Please forgive me, but please save me…he is mad. He will kill me!' Then, with the sound of a door at the end of the carriage crashing open, her terror returned. She forced her way past Zaharoff into the compartment.

While she cowered in his compartment, Zaharoff's bodyguard was wrestling with a man who was sporting a jewel-encrusted dagger. His face, contorted with fury, was half crushed by the bodyguard's other arm. Suddenly, his body went limp and he slithered toward the floor. Released from the bodyguard's grip he looked up in bewilderment. Without any resistance he allowed the conductor and the bodyguard to take him back to his compartment.

Zaharoff turned to the girl and in

his renowned, calm voice invited her to rest in his compartment until he could make arrangements for her to stay in a vacant compartment and to be guarded against any further attacks. Despite her shock, Zaharoff could see she was grateful for his intervention and kindness.

It was this brief encounter that would prove to be the first meeting of Zaharoff and the Spanish Duchess Maria, who was in fact on her honeymoon. Her assailant was the bridegroom, Don Francisco Principe de Bourbon y Bourbon, by birthright the Duke of Marchena and cousin of Alfonso XII.

Free from the shackles of her unstable, and later proved to be insane, young husband, the Duchess accompanied Zaharoff on his myriad of interminable journeys across Europe. But she was expected to be discreet when travelling with him. Maria never accompanied him to official receptions so as not to risk offending the Spanish court. Whenever on board the train, he was always in compartment seven, she in number eight.

Their relationship produced

three daughters. Sadly, one died in childhood; while the other two went on to marry an American shipowner and a Russian Count. In fact the Count became Zaharoff's resident agent in Istanbul and accumulated a large fortune.

However, as there was no divorce in Catholic Spain, Maria and Zaharoff could not marry. Also, by Spanish law, the couple's offspring were legally the offspring of the insane Duke.

But despite this, their relationship was one saturated by love on both sides. Zaharoff never went anywhere without a sepia-coloured picture of Maria and his three daughters in his wallet.

In 1923, Zaharoff bought the prestigious Monte Carlo casino for one million pounds and revelled in the knowledge that while the Grimaldi family ruled Monaco, he would in practice be the unofficial king, as whoever owned the casino and ancillary enterprises – the independent country's sole source of revenue – would be its monarch, his wife the regal consort.

Six months after purchasing the casino, Zaharoff learned of the death of Maria's ex-husband, Don Francisco. Maria explained to her lover that etiquette demanded that a year should elapse before she remarried. However, nine weeks before the period of mourning was due to elapse, Zaharoff persuaded Maria to legitimise their relationship. They were married quietly in the French town of Arronville on 22 September 1924.

For the next 18 months the couple lived a life of wonderful happiness. As a journey into nostalgia rather than a honeymoon, he took his bride to Paris and then on to the *Orient Express* to Vienna. And this time they both shared compartment number seven.

Unfortunately, the trip to Vienna was not a success as the city held too many sad memories for Maria of her previous honeymoon. The couple returned to France for a short while, before they moved on to Monte Carlo. It was there on 25 February 1926, that Lady Zaharoff, uncrowned queen of Monaco, died after a brief illness. Her husband was devastated.

Two days after the funeral he left Monte Carlo for Milan. He arrived 15 minutes before the *Orient Express*

Far Left: Alfonso XII.

left on its eastbound run. As usual compartment number seven had been reserved for him. The moment he was aboard, the compartment was locked and the blinds drawn.

In the early hours of the night, the car attendant was summoned by Zaharoff to inform him of the exact time. Upon being told it was exactly half past two he made sure the attendant left the compartment immediately as it was at 2.32am that the frantic scream and call for help had rung out, changing his life forever.

When his secretary cautiously knocked on his door just after dawn and, after getting no reply, entered his compartment, he saw Zaharoff sitting there bolt upright and the compartment was extremely cold. He had turned off the heating.

He never travelled on the *Orient Express* again. He returned to Monte Carlo by sea from Athens to Naples and then by train from Rome to Monte Carlo.

As the days and nights passed, he became more and more of a recluse. Rumours about his death flew about feverishly for three years, before a new (and more ruthless) wielder of power began striding the map of Europe Zaharoff had once trodden with impunity: Adolf Hitler.

With Hitler on the scene, no one was aware that on a winter's day in 1936, a convoy of cars left his home of Chateau Balincourt for Monte Carlo. His arrival at the Hotel de Paris went discreetly unannounced. The man who had once owned Monte Carlo was back again and no one knew it.

He died in his hotel suite on 27 November 1936. Before any announcement was made, his body was taken back to the Chateau and a private funeral in the grounds saw his body laid beside his wife's. His two daughters, a son-in-law and his secretary were the only mourners.

The following evening, on the last order of his master, his loyal bodyguard boarded the *Orient Express* at the Gare de l'Est, carrying an envelope containing the photograph which he, Zaharoff, had carried in his wallet for nearly 50 years. As the train approached Salzburg, the bodyguard tore up the photograph and scattered the pieces out of the window of compartment number seven...at exactly 2.32am.

Far Left: Adolf Hitler.

The Orient Express
on Page and Screen

There is little doubt that no form of public transportation has managed to garner the same amount of attention from writers in the way that the *Orient Express* managed. From the luxurious and sumptuous elegance of the train itself to the vast array of decadent and diverse members of society that travelled on it, the train has forever cast a spell on writers and readers alike.

The Stamboul Train and Murder on the Orient Express

Aside from the train's obvious glitz and glamour, the one undeniable facet that this unique train had going for it was the potential for gripping stories, primarily because it boasted the same facet that desert islands, prison and haunted houses had going for them: a place of no escape. And no story took better advantage of this fascinating notion than Agatha Christie's celebrated crime novel *Murder on the Orient Express*.

One of the most famous detective stories of all time, *Murder on the Orient Express* came out two years after Graham Greene's lauded *Stamboul Train* was published in 1932. Greene's novel was a fascinating examination of the clash of people of vastly different background

and character brought together by circumstance. Thanks to Greene's superb storytelling and sense of high adventure and insight, the book garnered superb reviews and large sales.

However, the train in Greene's story only ran for part of the journey as the *Orient Express*, but it is testimony to the author's ability to create such realism in his stories that the book expertly conveys the excitement and sense of glamour experienced by the train's passengers.

The book transformed both Greene's poor financial situation (he was in debt to his publishers, Heinemann) and his reputation with the critics after *The Man of Action* had failed to set the literary world alight. *Stamboul Train* continues to fly off the shelves today, 80 years on from its publication.

Agatha Christie was a regular traveller on the *Orient Express*, accompanying her first husband, Colonel Archibald Christie, to and from the Middle East. Her husband, after serving in the Royal Flying Corps during the First World War, spent much of his later life as a senior officer in British Intelligence. As a result, his wife managed to glean a plethora of real-life secret service plots, which she used as backgrounds for some

of her thrillers.

As a direct result of her trips on board this iconic train, she was able to write a successful detective story in which the train's background and the railroad on which it travels are faultless in terms of accuracy.

The sleeping car on the Istanbul-Calais section of the *Orient Express* presented a perfect background for the story. Christie had first-hand experience of what journeying in the carriage was like from her many experiences on it after a tiring trip from Syria on the *Taurus Express*, which ran from Baghdad via Ankara and Adana, arriving in Istanbul two hours before the *Orient Express*'s departure.

Christie's meticulous study of the *Orient Express*'s first stage of the east-west route and of the train's actual layout, down to the location of the toilet and the conductor's seat at the end of the corridor, gives the reader an image of almost photographic accuracy.

The quiet, yet ferociously insightful Belgian detective, Hercule Poirot, was Christie's most delightful creation and in many ways was the alter ego of the author. Through Poirot Christie could successfully cover any discussion

Left: Agatha Christie.

of masculine strength by making her protagonist shy and quite old, placing emphasis on his famous "little grey cells" to outwit the guilty.

Poirot made his debut in *The Mysterious Affair at Styles*, published in 1920, and it was clear from this impressive first work that wherever the diminutive detective went mysteries had to be solved.

In fact, Christie's innate ability to create an array of characters who were utterly believable and seemingly innocent, but could also be possibly guilty, is what makes this – as with all other Christie's novels – a classic of this or any other genre.

In the story there are 15 passengers: one detective, one future murder victim and the ominous 13 suspects. As the passengers are enjoying lunch, Poirot's "little grey cells" begin to examine them. At the table across the aisle sit three men – a large Italian, an expressionless Englishman, and an American in a "loud suit". Beyond them, sitting by herself, is a Russian princess. At a large table are three women – a pretty English girl, an elderly American lady and an apparently harmless middle-aged woman, while also sitting alone is a military looking gentleman.

Then, at the far end of the dining car is a lady's maid, an animated couple (presumably newlyweds) and finally two men, an American tycoon named Ratchett and his personal secretary. Ratchett appears to be superficially a bland old man but Poirot notices his "small and crafty" eyes that belie this assumption. The identity of the victim is left in no doubt. Ratchett is to die later that night, the victim of multiple stab wounds.

As for the unusual premise that leads to the murder itself (a man safely ensconced in a first-class sleeping berth on the world's most carefully controlled train), the simple solution would be that of someone boarding the train somewhere, hiding themselves in some nook and leaping from the train without injuring himself, before disappearing into a random Balkan town.

However, Christie was well aware of the midwinter Balkan conditions, as her trips on the *Orient Express* tended to be in the colder months. Thus, she cleverly utilised a situation that she knew frequently occurred – a complete stoppage when the train ran into a snow drift and the delay until the snow ploughs could clear the track.

The book was a massive success and its subsequent big screen adaptation was the first of a number of "all-star" adaptations of Agatha Christie novels in the 1970s and early 1980s. The original – and best – of the many adaptations was Sidney Lumet's multi-Academy Award-nominated film, whose tagline was: 'The greatest cast of suspicious characters ever involved in murder.'

From Paul Dehn and an uncredited Anthony Shaffer's screenplay, the film – like the book – features the Belgian super sleuth Hercule Poirot. *Murder on the Orient Express* stars Albert Finney as Poirot and the all-star suspects under suspicion include Lauren Bacall, Ingrid Bergman (delivering an Oscar-winning performance), Sean Connery, Sir John Gielgud, Vanessa Redgrave, Michael York and Anthony Perkins.

Richard Rodney Bennett's memorable *Orient Express* theme has been reworked into an orchestral suite and performed and recorded several times. It was performed on the original soundtrack album by the Orchestra of the Royal Opera House, Covent Garden under Marcus Dods. The piano soloist was the composer himself.

The Lady Vanishes

The Wheel Spins written by Ethel Lina White was to become the basis of the first – and some believe the best – movie featuring the train. The Balkans provided the background for this gripping story about Iris Carr, an attractive, rich, independent woman who has opted for an obscure resort for a vacation. Iris suffers sunstroke while waiting at the station to catch her train back to England.

It is an ominous beginning to what will be a very disturbing trip. On board, the still-dazed Iris befriends Mrs. Froy, a fellow Englishwoman who is a little eccentric, but who seems mostly agreeable and benign. However, with the train in motion, the enigmatic Froy mysteriously disappears while Iris is asleep. Her inexplicable departure throws Iris into a mind-bending mystery that will make her question both her sanity and the designs of the people around her.

Alfred Hitchcock, already a master at keeping moviegoers on the edge of their seats, bought the film rights to White's novel and placed the job of adapting the book for the big screen to two British writers, Frank Launder and Sidney Gilliatt.

The writers were no strangers to trainbound mysteries themselves, having penned *Seven Sinners* in 1936. Indeed, the two most memorable characters in this enduringly enjoyable Hitchcock classic (who were not in the novel), Charters and Caldicott, were inspired by Gordon Harker's golf obsessive in *Rome Express* and the corset salesman that Robert Donat encountered en route to Scotland in Hitchcock's *The 39 Steps*.

Although Hitchcock managed to recreate the excitement of travelling on the *Orient Express*, many of the sets were mock-ups, as the political situation of the time made filming on the train difficult and extreme risky. However, the film was one of the first major productions to exploit the public's fascination with transcontinental travel and was released to coincide with the Munich Crisis. The train-drama movie had come of age.

The film proved a major success on both sides of the Atlantic and was instrumental in securing Hitchcock an invitation to work in Hollywood, from where the legendary director never looked back. Without *The Lady Vanishes*, it is safe to assume we may have never had *Psycho, Vertigo, Rear Window* and *The Birds*.

From Russia, with Love

If *Murder on the Orient Express* provided a peerless description of the train in the 1930s, then Ian Fleming's seminal James Bond thriller, written in 1956, is easily one of the most accurate records of the train in its post-war incarnation.

The book (and indeed the subsequent film memorably starring Sean Connery as Agent 007) is possibly the most loved, and certainly most critically acclaimed, of all Fleming's Bonds and it enjoyed mammoth global sales. Much of the background to Fleming's stories – a man who enjoyed the finer things in life, courtesy of his upbringing in a wealthy family – came from his previous work in the Naval Intelligence Division or to events he knew of from the Cold War.

The plot of *From Russia, with Love* uses a fictional Soviet Spektor decoding machine as a lure to trap Bond, a machine which had its roots in the German Second World War Enigma machine.

The novel also used Fleming's knowledge to help create the plot device of spies on board the *Orient*

Left: Ethel Lina White.

Right: Similar to machine used in From Russia With Love.

LITTLE BOOK OF THE **ORIENT EXPRESS**

Express. Fleming knew of the story of Eugene Karp, a US naval attaché and intelligence agent based in Budapest who, in February 1950, took the *Orient Express* from Budapest to Paris, carrying a number of papers about blown US spy networks in the Eastern Bloc. Soviet assassins were already on the train. The conductor was drugged and Karp's body was found shortly afterwards in a railway tunnel south of Salzburg.

In the novel, Bond boards the *Orient Express* with Tatiana Romanova, an attractive Russian girl, unaware that she works for SMERSH, the clandestine Russian espionage organisation. As a result, the journey is fraught with the possibility of murder, mystery and treachery.

Bond's nemesis, Red Grant (immortalised by Robert Shaw in the film version), boards the train at Zagreb, pretending to be agent Nash from "Station 'Y'". He drugs Romanova at dinner, and then overcomes Bond. Grant taunts Agent 007, boasting that SPECTRE has been pitting the Soviets and the British against each other, and claims that Romanova thinks that "she's doing it all for mother Russia", when she is in fact working for SPECTRE.

Bond tricks Grant into opening Bond's attaché case, detonating its tear gas booby trap in his face. This allows Bond to attack him, and the ensuing struggle is still one of cinema's greatest fights and a thrilling end to Bond's adventure on board the world's most famous train.

There is little doubt that without such a richly conceived scene both the book and the film wouldn't have captured the imagination as they did. Even today, many years later aficionados and fans alike, still cite the film as the benchmark from which all Bonds should be judged.

What's more, it should be noted that the most glowing recommendation comes from perhaps the greatest Bond of all, the original 007, Sean Connery, who has never deviated from his opinion that *From Russia, with Love* is the finest of them all.

An interesting postscript to the link between Fleming and the *Orient Express* comes from Lieutenant Commander Merlin Minshall, who in his book *Guilt Edged* describes how he killed a "beautiful Nazi spy" on the Simplon *Orient Express*. Minshall – an officer of British naval intelligence, whose operation chief during the war was none other than Fleming himself – claimed to have survived two attempts by German agents to kill him, before killing the German in the corridor and bundling the body out of a toilet window.

This story was questioned by one of his former colleagues, Lieutenant Commander Michael Henry Mason, a man of many talents and one who claimed it was in fact he who dispatched not one but two German agents. His claim was backed up by Sir Alexander Glen, who during the war also occupied a high position in naval intelligence.

One thing's for sure, at least some of the "true" stories about *Murder on the Orient Express* were more thrilling than fiction.

Lady Chatterley's Lover

The stream of novels boasting plots involving the *Orient Express*'s passengers achieved massive popularity that coincided with the train's most celebrated period – the period of time between the two world wars.

First published in 1928 – and banned in Britain for more than 30 years – D.H. Lawrence's famous novel sees Connie (Lady Chatterley) embark on a passionate affair with her husband's gamekeeper Oliver Mellors.

Lady Chatterley's husband has been paralysed in a war accident and his emotional neglect of Connie forces distance between the couple. It is this neglect and subsequent sexual frustration that leads Connie into an affair with Mellors.

When Mellors' wife returns to him, Lady Chatterley goes to Venice with her sister. Her father, Sir Malcolm Reid – a veteran artist, arranges to take his daughter back to England and to her impotent husband on board the *Orient Express*. While on board the train, Connie tells her father that she is pregnant, much to his delight, unaware that Mellors is the child's father.

'The old artist always did himself well,' Lawrence wrote. 'He took berths on the Orient Express, in spite of Connie's dislike of *trains de luxe*, the atmosphere of vulgar depravity there is aboard them nowadays.'

To Lawrence, the *Orient Express* – the means of transportation for the wealthy and the decadent, was the ideal location

for contrasting the hypocrisy of her father with the honesty of his heroine. However, the unfortunate irony for Lawrence was that the only people able to buy the French-printed edition of the book were precisely those he meant to vilify.

The novel was the reading matter of many *Orient Express* travellers as they embarked on an illicit adventure. However, the plethora of well-thumbed copies were eventually destroyed due to the risk of discovery by Customs at the British port of entry.

Time, and a change in people's perception of the novel, saw the story become more culturally acceptable. In the United States, the free publication of *Lady Chatterley's Lover* was a significant event in the "sexual revolution". At the time, the book was a topic of widespread discussion and a byword of sorts.

Meanwhile, the book was seen as sufficiently safe in Britain to be parodied on the *Morecambe and Wise* show. A "play what Ernie wrote", *The Handyman and M'Lady*, was based on it, with Michele Dotrice as the Lady Chatterley figure. Introducing it, Ernie explained that his play was 'about a man who has an accident with a combine harvester, which unfortunately makes him impudent.'

La Madonne des Sleepings (The Madonna of the Sleeping Cars)

Written by Maurice Dekobra, this novel was enormously popular before, during, and for some years after the Second World War. Debroka, a Parisian born in 1888, began his professional career as a foreign correspondent, before turning his hand to fiction writing. Amongst his prodigious output of work was *La Madonne des Sleepings*, almost certainly the best known of his myriad works.

This story first appeared in 1927 and focused on a story of romance and intrigue set against the backdrop of the *Orient Express* route. The book's appeal to those masses ravaged by the world depression and inevitable onset of war, was the clash between the last survivors of European aristocracy and Russia's clandestine secret agents, all brought face to face by the *Orient Express*.

The story's heroine is Lady Diana Wynham, whose love of travel and the

regular schedules of the decadent *Orient Express* form the backdrop to this story of amorous adventures and melodrama.

However, Debroka's characters were always deliberately written in a fantastical way. It was the publication of Greene's *Stamboul Train* in 1932, which would finally put the reader in the path of characters that readers could genuinely relate to and to put them in the exciting situation of actually travelling together on this most iconic of trains.

Centre: A passenger boards the Orient Express during its journey through Yugoslavia on its way to Istanbul.

A Sense of Adventure – Espionage and Intrigue on the Orient Express

There is something about train travel, and the *Orient Express* in particular, which is redolent of intrigue and adventure, perhaps it is the plethora of different carriages and separate compartments. A magnate for secret agents, both real and fictional, the train attracted many secretive individuals.

Mata Hari

Margaretha Gertrud Zelle, better known as Mata Hari, the most dangerous spy on the globe, travelled on board the *Orient Express* during the *belle époque*, contributing greatly to the popular moniker of the train as the "mystery train".

Born in Holland in 1876, Margaretha was married at 19 to an officer in the Dutch Colonial Army, whose family was of Scottish descent. For her it was a marriage of convenience. Her mother had died years earlier and her father was bankrupt, so the opportunity to escape her penniless life and instead enjoy a secure life in Java where her husband was stationed was too good to pass up.

However, her husband was a drunk and a few years later the couple returned to Holland on a miniscule pension. Unsurprisingly, the marriage broke down and Margaretha decided to move to Paris in search of a life of adventure. Soon she was in the company of many male friends, most elderly, who all kept

her comfortable. She may have lived happily with this lifestyle, had someone not suggested she become a dancer.

Despite no dance training whatsoever, she presented herself to Guimet, the owner of the Oriental Museum, where Indian and Arabian dancing ensembles occasionally staged performances. When she was in Java she had often watched Oriental ritual dancers, and so pretended to Guimet that she knew all about Hindu and Malayan dancing.

What impressed him was her offer to dance in the nude, the first woman ever to do so in Paris. He invented the name Mata Hari for her, which is Malayan for "eye of day". Despite her improvised

Right: Robert Baden-Powell.

routine, her success was instantaneous and soon she was the star of the Folies-Bergeres.

Her tours through Europe took her to Berlin, Madrid, Rome and many more of the continent's capitals. And it was on these tours that she acquired a considerable number of distinguished and influential lovers. These included the French ambassador Cambon, the composer Massenet and the German diplomat Baron von Krohn, who at the beginning of the First World War became one of the chiefs of the Kaiser's Secret Service.

It was on the behest of one of her friends, Baron Henri de Rothschild that she went to Vienna, travelling on the *Orient Express* as far as Bucharest. Unfortunately, it was her friendship with the Baron that would prove her downfall.

In 1916 she was in France when she decided to visit Madrid where von Krohn had set up a German espionage outpost. Returning from Spain to Holland, she was taken off a ship at Falmouth on the suspicion of being a German spy. British intelligence decided to let her go as there was no evidence that she had obtained any secrets. But when she returned to France, spy mania was rampant. She was arrested, tried and sentenced to death.

One of the biggest accusations against her was that she seduced the French War Minister Messimy into betraying war secrets, which she was supposed to have communicated to von Krohn. She was executed by firing squad in 1917, but the Mata Hari myth lingered. It became one of the classic espionage stories even if it is exceptionally doubtful whether she was even an effective spy.

Robert Baden-Powell

One of the characters well known to the personnel of the *Orient Express* during the last decade of the nineteenth century was a gaunt, coy Englishman who was to go on to enjoy worldwide fame in a much different sphere: Robert Baden-Powell.

The sleeping car attendants would arrange that this unassuming character had a compartment all to himself, simply because he insisted on the heating being turned off and the windows lowered

Above: The *Orient Express* interior.

even in winter and bad weather.

Unsurprisingly this passenger was thought of as an English eccentric. The fact that he always carried with him paraphernalia such as preserving jars, nets, sketching pads (the equipment of an enthusiastic butterfly collector) only served to support this theory.

Baden-Powell was in his early thirties when he started to travel on the world's most famous train, boasting a heavy tan thanks to his military service in Afghanistan and India. After 1887, he was given leave by the British Army to indulge his passion for butterflies. However, the man who was to go on to enjoy worldwide fame as the founder of the Boy Scout movement was in fact an intelligence agent, a career move he would document years later in his book,

My Adventures as a Spy in 1915.

The reason for his cover as a lepidopterist was simple. Any butterfly lover would have confirmed that to seek new specimens for his collections he had to explore those areas forbidden to the general public where the butterflies by day, and the moths by night, could flourish without molestation.

Fortification zones were his targets and he was able to roam around the Dalmatian Coast making drawings of naval installations at Ragusa, Spalato and the Bay of Cattaro, sometimes aided by friendly Austrian police and naval guards intrigued by this eccentric Englishman.

Many admired his drawings of butterflies but the simple fact was that the drawings of blobs, lines and squiggles of the butterflies' wings actually formed a colour-coded plan of fortifications, to be redrawn to scale at a later date.

As it was not the best idea to trespass on Russian territory, the site of one of his earliest assignments, Baden-Powell transferred his explorations to Austria-Hungary and the Balkan countries (including Turkey), the lands that the *Orient Express* conveniently provided a ready means of entry, and if needs be, exit.

Baden-Powell's drawings proved to be of inestimable value when the First World War broke out and enabled Britain and Italian warships to pinpoint their targets – an incredible achievement that many of his scout disciples would agree amounts to something that no number of his badges could ever pay tribute to.

American agents

In the decade up to the First World War, the United States had no institutionalised secret service at all, and agents of the State and War departments sent to Europe used the *Orient Express* routes as diplomats and military attaches.

However, after 1919, following the enormous development in the oil-producing areas of the Middle East and the realignment of power blocs, US finance poured in to exploit mineral and natural resources. The investments needed protection and so Washington began to collate information on both the political and economic fronts.

The intelligence activities were uncoordinated and so British tactics were adopted, with people such as archaeologists and newspaper men working as amateur but effective operators in the field, and of the most colourful of these agents was Reuben Markham. He would drop off the *Orient Express* at various Balkan stations to preach Christianity to a disinterested and sometimes hostile population of orthodox Christians and Muslims.

Many US agents became high ranking officers of the OSS when it was formed at the inception of the Second World War. David Bruce, the distinguished American diplomat, who was ambassador to France, West Germany and Britain during his political tenure, was recommended for espionage services by Allen Dulles (who would go on to be the longest serving Director of the CIA) after serving in France in 1918. His duties required him to journey on the *Orient Express* several times, with his Colt .45 strapped to his hip.

US agents, generously supplied with funds, were regarded by the *Orient Express*'s personnel as "Yankee business millionaires" because of the large tips they left. This cover was extremely useful for the agents, which some of the top CIA operators, including Colonel Meade or Kermit "Kim" Roosevelt, gladly accepted.

The era of the secret agent following his own hunches and sporting a disguise is, much like the *Orient Express* itself, a chapter consigned to history. But before technology, different methodology, and in-depth training became the norm, this method of intelligence was invaluable and in many ways prevented catastrophe on a global scale.

ALSO AVAILABLE IN THE LITTLE BOOK SERIES

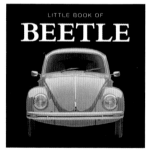

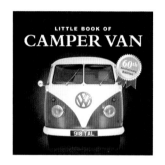

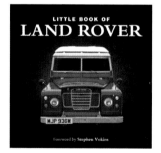

ALSO AVAILABLE IN THE LITTLE BOOK SERIES

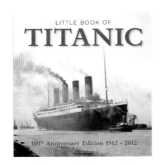

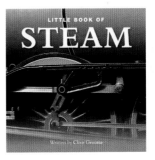

The pictures in this book were provided courtesy of the following:

WIKIMEDIA COMMONS

Design & Artwork: SCOTT GIARNESE

Published by: DEMAND MEDIA LIMITED & G2 ENTERTAINMENT LIMITED

Publishers: JASON FENWICK & JULES GAMMOND

Written by: ANDREW O'BRIEN